INSIGHT GUIDES

BILBAO

POCKET GUIDE

C000066413

PLAN & BOOK
YOUR TAILOR-MADE TRIP

 **BRAZIL**  **CHILE**  **ECUADOR**

TAILOR-MADE TRIPS & UNIQUE EXPERIENCES CREATED BY LOCAL TRAVEL EXPERTS AT INSIGHTGUIDES.COM/HOLIDAYS

Insight Guides has been inspiring travellers with high-quality travel content for over 45 years. As well as our popular guidebooks, we now offer the opportunity to book tailor-made private trips completely personalised to your needs and interests. By connecting with one of our local experts, you will directly benefit from their expertise and local know-how, helping you create memories that will last a lifetime.

HOW INSIGHTGUIDES.COM/HOLIDAYS WORKS

STEP 1

Pick your dream destination and submit an enquiry, or modify an existing itinerary if you prefer.

STEP 2

Fill in a short form, sharing details of your travel plans and preferences with a local expert.

STEP 3

Your local expert will create your personalised itinerary, which you can amend until you are completely satisfied.

STEP 4

Book securely online. Pack your bags and enjoy your holiday! Your local expert will be available to answer questions during your trip.

BENEFITS OF PLANNING & BOOKING AT
INSIGHTGUIDES.COM/HOLIDAYS

PLANNED BY LOCAL EXPERTS
The Insight Guides local experts are hand-picked, based on their experience in the travel industry and their impeccable standards of customer service.

SAVE TIME & MONEY
When a local expert plans your trip, you save time and money when you book, even during high season. You won't be charged for using a credit card either.

TAILOR-MADE TRIPS
Book with Insight Guides, and you will be in complete control of the planning process, from the initial selections to amending your final itinerary.

BOOK & TRAVEL STRESS-FREE
Enjoy stress-free travel when you use the Insight Guides secure online booking platform. All bookings come with a money-back guarantee.

WHAT OTHER TRAVELLERS THINK ABOUT TRIPS
BOOKED AT INSIGHTGUIDES.COM/HOLIDAYS

Trip to Vietnam

The organization was superb, the drivers professional, and accommodation quite comfortable. I was well taken care of! My thanks to your colleagues who helped make my trip to Vietnam such a great experience. My only regret is that I couldn't spend more time in the country.

Heather   ★★★★★

TOP 10 ATTRACTIONS

MUSEO GUGGENHEIM
The symbol of the regenerated city.
See page 50.

PUENTE BIZKAIA
Take the high level walkway
across the river. See page 59.

CASCO VIEJO
A dense cluster of old streets around the
cathedral. See page 29.

ARTXANDA FUNICULAR
Take this quaint inclined railway
up the hillside. See page 55.

AZKUNA ZENTROA
Warehouse-turned-arts-and-entertainment-centre. See page 42.

PINTXOS BARS
Tapas are taken to another gourmet level. See page 103.

SAN JUAN DE GAZTELUGATXE
The most spectacular sight on the Basque Coast. See page 62.

SAN SEBASTIÁN
An elegant holiday resort built around a perfect crescent shaped beach. See page 70.

CAFÉ IRUÑA
Drop into this classic Bilbao bar. See page 111.

MUSEO DE BELLAS ARTES
The city's celebrated fine arts museum. See page 81.

A PERFECT DAY

8am

Breakfast with the best view

Many bars and cafés don't open early and your best option for breakfast is in a hotel. If money is no object, have breakfast on the terrace of the Gran Hotel Domine, with its incomparable view of the Guggenheim. If you want something cheaper, go up to Alameda Mazarredo to Sua San at No 79.

10am

River cruising

Spend the morning actively getting a feel for Bilbao. The best way to do that is to make for the waterside, the ria. Visit the Maritime Museum and then take to the water itself either in a canoe, a self-drive motor boat or on a guided river tour. Alternatively, hire bikes or ebikes and cycle down one river bank, cross over and poodle back along the other.

2pm

Lunchtime

Whether you choose wheels or water, that should see you nicely to lunchtime – which you can put off until 2 or 3pm. Etxanobe Euskalduna has tremendous views and excellent food but it can be pricey. If you want less fuss, you can eat just as well in the Ensanche where there are plenty of restaurants, notably El Globo, which will serve you pintxos or something more substantial.

4pm

Afternoon in the Old Quarter

Walk or catch a bus or metro to the Casco Viejo. Stroll along small streets, browse in interesting shops and take time in particular to visit the cathedral and the Basque Museum.

IN **BILBAO**

7pm

Pintxos in the Plaza
When you have done enough walking and sightseeing retreat to Plaza Nueva for the pintxos you have earned. Ideally you'll get there before the after-work crowds and find a seat or standing room in Víctor Montes. If that is full, almost any other bar will do – Gure Toki for instance or Café Bar (see page 109). Serious tapas-hoppers would do all three.

11pm

Night out
At 11pm the night is only just beginning and it is time to seek out some entertainment. Bilbao has bars galore offering cocktails and live music. The Casco Viejo is one good place to be, or you could cross the bridge beside the church of San Anton to see if there is a band playing at Bilborock.

9:30pm

Dinner
Plaza Nueva is a good place to stay for dinner (which you will have reserved). If you want to shift location, Mandoya is not far away, and is good for either modern or traditional Basque cuisine.

6pm

Merienda
Tea-time in Spain is called *merienda*: a late afternoon pause for coffee and a cake. Café Bizuete is a good place to stop for a respite.

CONTENTS

INTRODUCTION

Few cities in the world have undergone a metamorphosis as dramatic as that of Bilbao. For centuries, this was an industrial city characterized by the grime, smog and residues of heavy industry; but when the shipbuilding yards and steel mills became uncompetitive and fell into decline at the end of the 20th century, the decision was taken to reinvent Bilbao as a city of services and art. A time traveller from even 30 years ago wouldn't recognize the vibrant, cosmopolitan, cultural city of today.

THE GUGGENHEIM EFFECT

Emblematic of the transformation of Bilbao is one unmissable building, the **Museo Guggenheim**, which transformed a dock-side wasteland into a cutting edge contemporary art space and major tourist attraction. The arrival of Frank Gehry's extraordinary structure at the end of the last millennium triggered a string of visionary projects that have led to Bilbao becoming a showcase of international avant garde architecture. At the same time, old Bilbao was treated to a facelift. The atmospheric Casco Viejo underwent its own renaissance as buildings were cleaned and streets were pedestrianized; and museums were brought up to date. What characterises contemporary Bilbao

Need a lift?

With a steep slope in every direction, Bilbao depends on its 21 vertical or inclined lifts to save legwork. All but two of them are free to use. The only ones you are likely to need for sightseeing are the Arxanda funicular and the Ascensor Mallona in Casco Viejo metro station.

is the exciting way that the ancient meets the cutting edge; the traditional mercantile interacts with the digital age. Nowhere is this seen to better effect than in the Alhondiga, a warehouse re-baptised as Azkuna Zentro, an arts, entertainment and sports centre where people of all ages like to hang out. All of this redevelopment stimulated – and continues to – an exciting, entrepreneurial human

Colourful apartments

atmosphere which has resulted in Bilbao being a favourite place for creative types to set up shops, bars, restaurants and boutique hotels.

LOOKING DOWN

If you want an overview of the city, it is surprisingly easy to walk out of the busy streets with their high-rise modern architecture and discover open, green spaces with a view. The most convenient way to do this is to take the quaint funicular railway up to the summit of Mount Artxanda (300m).

Looking down from this point, the first thing you notice is that on three sides the urban area is hemmed in by low but steep-sided green hills, creating the effect of its tower blocks and other buildings being enclosed in a natural bowl. For this reason, Bilbainos affectionately refer to their city as "El Botxo" ("the hole").

Athletic Bilbao fans

You also can't help but notice that the city straggles down river as a conurbation that stretches for 10km to the sea at Santzurzi, the biggest port on the coast of Northern Spain.

This river is important in itself. It physically divides the city in two but also symbolically unites it. Confusingly, you may see or hear it referred to by one several names. It is sometimes called the River Nervion-Ibaizabal, which is what it is but it is most commonly known as the Ria de Bilbao, as it is technically the upper part of a ria, or tidal inlet, of the Cantabrian sea.

MEET THE BASQUES

The conurbation of Bilbao is home to a million people, nearly half the population of the Basque Country, an autonomous region of Spain with its own strong sense of autonomy and identity.

The Basqueness of Bilbao cannot be overemphasized. You see it everywhere, not least in the bilingual street names. But don't worry: Bilbao has never been a closed city and its long history of being open to the outside world through trade is one reason for its current success. The Basques of Bilbao are proud of their language and their culture but they'll happily speak to you in Spanish, or English if they can.

The Basques trace their history back to the proverbial mists of time and they have preserved their singular traditions intact. The best of these – including extraordinary trials of strength and endurance – can be seen in Bilbao's hugely energetic summer festival, the Great Week.

If you want to start a conversation with almost any local, just ask them how the Basques differ from the rest of the Spanish population. Better still, express an interest in the local football

⊙ THE BASQUE COUNTRIES

The Basque Country is an official region of Spain – the Comunidad Autónoma del País Vasco, or Eusakdi (in Basque). This is made up of three provinces: Bizkaia (around Bilbao), Gupuzkoa (around San Sebastián) and Araba (around Vitoria).

In its wider, ethnic meaning, the term "Basque Country" includes the separate province of Navarra (around Pamplona) and the south-western corner of France extending inland from Biarritz and Bayonne – although the French Basque Country has no official status of its own.

The Basques have their own culture and their unique language, which is widely spoken but almost everyone you meet will be bilingual and happy to talk to you in Spanish (which they call Castellano – Castilian).

Many people in the País Vasco (but by no means all) identify as Basque rather than Spanish and you should be careful to respect the difference. While the region has great autonomy over its affairs under the constitution, there is a vociferous minority that would like to see the Basque Country become an independent state.

team, the prodigiously successful Athletic Bilbao, which has its own cult following.

STRANGERS WELCOME

Around 3.5 million tourists visit Bilbao annually, by numerous international flights into the airport or on the ferry from Britain that docks at Santurzi.

⊙ THE BASQUE LANGUAGE

Of Western Europe's living languages, only Euskera (Basque) does not belong to the Indo-European family. It has fascinated linguists since the Middle Ages, when scholars traced it to Tubal, the grandson of Noah who settled the peninsula after the Flood. More recently, philologists comparing the Basque words for axe, aitzor, and stone, aitz, have raised the possibility that the language dates from a time when tools were made of stone.

Throughout history, Basque has been more an oral language than a written one. There is an inscription in Basque dating from the 1st century AD but the first book entirely in Euskera wasn't published until the mid-16th century and the first novel only appeared in 1898, coincidental with the rise of nationalism. According to the official estimates in around thirty percent of the population of the Basque Country are "actively bilingual", speaking Euskara as their first language but understanding Castilian.

Basque is widely taught in schools and enjoys an equal status with Castilian for official uses. For most speakers the language is a matter of cultural pride, but for a few it symbolises the political struggle for independence.

Visitors are drawn in by a city that combines extraordinary artistic activity with a variegated lifestyle that includes an enthusiasm for good food and drink. The pintxos (tapas) served by Bilbao's bars are legendary.

If there is a downside, the locals are used to it. The humid oceanic climate guarantees a fair amount of rain, especially between October and April, but it also moderates the tem-

Zumaia cliffs and beach

peratures to an average of 8 degrees in winter and 20 degrees in summer.

If you don't mind the odd shower, Bilbao has one great advantage for the visitor. The city centre is flat on both sides of the river and its sights are often clustered together. There is an efficient public transport system if you need it, but you could get around quite easily on foot or by bike.

BEYOND BILBAO

You'll be hard pressed to squeeze the best of Bilbao into a week-end – even with good organisation and if you resist the temptation to hop from bar to bar – but if you have longer, you should consider taking a trip to the nearby beauty spots of the Basque coast. Other splendid day trips include the Rioja wine region and the sedate resort of San Sebastián, another coastal city, but in many ways the perfect complement to the bustle of Bilbao.

A BRIEF HISTORY

Starting from humble beginnings 800 years ago, Bilbao prospered as an industrial port and centre of international commerce. Despite periods of upheaval brought by war, world economic conditions forced it to reinvent itself at the approach of the new millennium into the lively cultural metropolis that it is today.

FOUNDING OF BILBAO

Until the 14th century, Bilbao was just another insignificant fishing village on the Atlantic coast of Spain – but it did have three significant advantages. It stood on a natural navigable inlet of the Atlantic, the Ibaizabal-Nervión estuary, where there was flat enough land to build docks for sea-going ships and the water deep enough to moor cargo vessels. In addition, its location meant that it could handle the increasing quantities of wool and other goods coming from Castile in central Spain. Thirdly, Bilbao stood over a rich deposit or iron ore – which will become important later in the story.

On 15 June 1300, Diego López V de Haro, feudal lord of the region of Biscay, recognized Bilbao's potential for economic development by granting it a charter so that it became officially a "villa", or a borough. This favoured status gave the port trading privileges, in particular exemption from paying customs tribute to the king of Spain. The city's founder is honoured by having the principle avenue named after him (Gran Vía de Don Diego López de Haro) and his statue stands in one of the main squares, Plaza Circular.

The original Bilbao was really two separate settlements facing each other across the water: the area known as Bilbao

16th century map of Bilbao

la Vieja (marked by the Muelle de La Merced and Muelle de Marzana) on the left bank and the Casco Viejo on the right. Two floods and a fire destroyed most of the earliest buildings in Bilbao, but remains of the old wall can be seen near the church of San Anton adjacent to the bridge of the same name. There are also remains of medieval buildings in two streets, Ronda and Barrencalle.

COMMERCIAL DEVELOPMENT IN THE 15TH TO 18TH CENTURIES

During the 15th century, Bilbao consolidated its commercial importance as its trading privileges were extended, making it the largest port in the territory of the Lordship of Biscay. It traded with other European ports and, in the decades after 1492, with the American colonies. It particularly handled shipments of iron.

The population expanded and the core of the Casco Viejo ("the seven streets") was laid out. The Gothic cathedral dedicated to Santiago (St James) was also erected, replacing an earlier chapel.

In 1511, the Consulate of the Sea Bilbao was created. This influential institution had jurisdiction over the commercial

⊘ THE ORIGIN OF THE BASQUES

The origins of the Basques remain mysterious. They are a distinct people, generally with a different build from the French and Spanish and a different blood-group distribution from the rest of Europe. Their language, the complex Euskara, is unrelated to any other, and was already spoken in Spain when Indo-European languages began to arrive three thousand years ago. Written records were scarce until the first books in Euskara were published in the mid-sixteenth century. Language and culture survived instead through oral traditions, including that of the bertsolariak popular poets specializing in improvised verse.

The Basque people have unquestionably inhabited the western Pyrenees for thousands of years. Archaeologists and anthropologists used to argue that they might be the last surviving representatives of Europe's first modern human population, Cro-Magnon hunter-gatherers. More recently, however, DNA analysis has demonstrated clear affinities between 5500-year-old skeletons found in El Portalón cave, near Burgos, and modern Basques. The new suggestion is that the Basques are descended from early Neolithic farmers who became isolated – perhaps through a deliberate retreat into the mountains – from subsequent waves of migration.

development of the estuary and its work helped Bilbao to become one of the most important ports in the newly unified Spain, a vital northern outlet for trade. It became the largest port on the Bay of Biscay.

The European economy suffered a crisis in the 17th century but Bilbao still thrived because it had attracted the business of large English and Dutch shipping companies. The growing city acquired grander streets lined with bourgeois houses and baroque churches. This phrase of the city's development was centred on Bidebarrieta, the "main street" of the time, connecting Correo with the Arenal.

Basques in 1800

WARS OF THE 19TH CENTURY

In the 19th century, Bilbao's prosperity was disrupted by war. The Peninsular War (1808–1813) brought Napoleon's troops to the Basque Country but Bilbao initially became a defiant pocket of resistance. Possession of it changed several times during the course of 1808. Soon after, the Basque Country was the principal theatre for the Carlist Wars that pitted Spaniards against each other during the early 19th century.

As the empire dwindled, Spain in the 19th century became an increasingly troubled place, a battleground for ideologists and vested interests. On the death of Fernando VII, extremist

Carlist horsemen

feelings were focused into support for rival contenders to the throne: either Isabel II or her uncle, Carlos. The supporters of the latter became known as "Carlists" and northern Spain was their stronghold. They were conservatives and their principal political ambition was the restoration of a strong monarchy – they disliked the idea of an elected parliament. They were also a staunchly pro-Catholic church, and pro the rights of landowner against peasant. They were suspicious of cities, industry and modernity in general, which they felt to be behind the discontent and freethinking that were plaguing Spain.

In their red berets, the Carlists are often depicted as romantic guerrillas fighting to bring back an old order in which everyone knew their place and was therefore at ease. They made their headquarters at Oñati (in the Basque Country) and Estella (Navarra), and fought three futile wars (1833–39, 1847–49 and 1872–76). In some ways, these conflicts between reformers and reactionary religious vested interests smouldered unresolved until they were reignited by the Civil War.

Being economically powerful and liberal-leaning, Bilbao was a target for reactionary forces. In 1835, General Tomás de Zumalacárregui unsuccessfully tried to take the city and the following year Baldomero Espartero similarly failed. Bilbao was besieged in April 1874 during the Third Carlist War but liberated by General Concha on 2 May of the same year.

INDUSTRALISATION

In spite of conservative resistance, Spain was modernising as fast as it could and Bilbao was the forefront of a late industrial revolution. The city had two great resources: its trading history as a port and its nearby mines. Bizkaia had prodigious

⊘ THE BOMBING OF GERNIKA

The name Gernika is famous around the world thanks to the nightmare painting by **Pablo Picasso**, *Guernica*, which commemorated its **saturation bombing** during the Spanish Civil War. In one of the first such raids ever perpetrated on a civilian centre, on April 27, 1937, planes from the Condor Legion, which had been lent to Franco by Hitler and had taken off from Vitoria-Gasteiz, obliterated 71 percent of the buildings in Gernika in the space of three hours.

Gernika was chosen as the target largely for its symbolic importance. Around 250 people died, many of whom were attending the weekly market that's still held every Monday in the Plaza de Gernika. The nearby town of Durango had been bombed a few days earlier, but because there were no foreign observers, the reports were simply not believed. While the German government acknowledged its involvement in the bombing in 1997, to this day the Spanish government has never admitted its role.

Picasso started work on his painting the day that news of the bombing reached him in Paris. Finally brought "home" to Spain after the death of Franco, it is now exhibited in the Centro de Arte Reina Sofía in Madrid.

A Novel Thought

"I remember the ships swinging up and down the Nervión– I watched them from my window. Ships of all the world…The slums, the old town, are an area of high built, narrow streets. They swarm with crowded life… the famous foundries… where the great fires never went out; where half naked men moved like unreal creatures through glare and darkness". Kate O'Brien, Irish novelist, 1937

deposits of iron ore that had possibly been exploited by the Romans and had certainly provided high quality steel for sword blades in the Middle Ages. Now, in the last half of the 19th century, the mines truly came into their own. The ore was low in phosphorus and well suited to the Bessemer steel-making process. Blast furnaces were built beside the ria. The coal needed to feed the fires was imported from Asturias (west of Bilbao) or from abroad.

Bilbao (and Spain in general) had two problems, however. One was that much of the capital for any development had to come from abroad – meaning that up to half the profits from any enterprise would be exported rather than spent locally. The other handicap was the lack of a market for the output of industry – vital for economic growth. Spain's empire had shrunk vastly since its heyday in the 17th century and it was Britain that supplied manufactured goods to developing countries in the Americas and Asia. Bilbao's industry, therefore, only succeeded to a limited extent and it was trade that continued to be the mainstay of the economy. In particular, most iron ore was exported rather than processed locally. At the end of the century Bizkaia was producing around a tenth of the world's total output of iron ore, all of it passing through the port of Bilbao.

THE HAVES AND THE HAVE NOTS OF PROGRESS

Mining and steelworking were dirty, difficult occupations for the ordinary workers but the owners of the pits and plants grew rich on the proceeds. The elite that had made its fortune on trade now ceded to an industrial bourgeoisie. Bilbao was transformed into a well-to-do port in one of Spain's principal centres of heavy engineering and shipbuilding. The heyday of the city's economic history at the end of the 19th century can be clearly seen in the grandiose buildings built along the Gran Vía.

On 1 March 1862, the railway reached Abando station, creating a fast new transport link with the rest of Spain. The influential Banco de Bilbao was founded in 1857 and the stock exchange inaugurated in 1890. The urban area was simultaneously transformed with promenades and broad, straight avenues lined with trees. Many of the most distinctive squares buildings of the city date from the late 19th century, including Plaza Nueva, the City Hall, the transporter bridge at Portugalete and the Arriaga Theatre – inspired by Paris's Opera House.

The late 19th century was also a time of rediscovery of cultures submerged into the Spanish

Blast Furnaces in Bilbao, painting from 1908

Recruitment poster for the Basque army which fought Franco's troops

VI ABEŔI-EGUN GUDARI

melting pot. Sabino Arana (born in Bilbao) almost single-hand-edly defined Basque nationalism, which would go onto create a huge impact on the 20th century.

20TH CENTURY

By the early 20th century, Bilbao had made itself the undis-puted industrial powerhouse of the Basque Country and one of the most important commercial centres of Spain. In 1900, the Euskalduna shipyards were founded (on the site what is now a conference centre of the same name) and in 1902, the blast furnaces of the Altos Hornos de Vizcaya (AHV) came into production. Bilbao was an enterprising, forward-looking cosmopolitan city, but it was not immune from the effects of the polarization that was taking place in national politics. This erupted in the Spanish Civil War (1936–9) when the right-wing military and Catholic fanatic General Franco rebelled against the elected government of the Republic. He was aided by armed forces supplied by Nazi Germany. Bilbao stayed loyal to the government but because of this it would find itself on the losing side of the war. The city was defended by the so-called "Iron Ring" of defences that surrounded Bilbao, the remains of which are still be seen in the Lezama mountains, but this wasn't enough to do more than delay the rebel forces.

On 31 August 1936, planes under Franco's command attacked, dropping eight bombs on the city. A few weeks later, on 25 September, Bilbao was shelled and the following day German planes attacked with incendiary bombs. As the principal port on the north coast still in the hands of the government, Bilbao was and important point of evacuation for civilians. Thousands of children were put on ships bound for England, Belgium and the Soviet Union, some never to return.

In May 1937, Bilbao came under siege by Franco's forces. It was bombed and shelled into submission. The war came to an end in 1939, with Franco victorious. He took his revenge on the Basque Country that had opposed him by suppressing its autonomy. In reaction, a tenacious terrorist organization, ETA, grew up in the Basque Country backed by a popular political movement. Both peaceful demonstrations and violent terrorist acts were

A Mountain Village

"The Basque is the man of the mountain village, and Bilbao is nothing more than an overgrown mountain village. The broken and hilly site is naturally picturesque, and the town seems to have reverently adapted itself to the sinuosities of its site, and to that extent only is it adequate and satisfying." Havelock Ellis, physician, 1908 all too common in the life of Bilbao in the last half of the 20th century.

Franco died in 1975 and Spain was swiftly and unsentimentally transformed into a democracy based on the equality and justice that had been missing for so long. A central tenet of the new constitution was restoring power over its own affairs to the long suffering Basque Country. Bilbao was politically reinvigorated – it saw many demonstrations by Basque nationalists during the 1980s – but economically it was in decline. Its old industries could not compete in the globalizing market place at the end of the 20th century. The 1973 Oil Crisis hit the shipbuilding business badly and competition from Asia finished off the Euskalduna yard in 1988 (not without trade union resistance) with the loss of 1,300 jobs. The steelworks were finally forced to close in 1996 but by that time a daring new plan for regenerating Bilbao was well under way.

THE TRANSFORMATION OF BILBAO

The future began early in Bilbao with the creation of an extraordinary building which would draw the world's attention to a hitherto unknown grimy, workaday city. In 1997 Frank Gehry's titanium-clad Guggenheim building opened its doors.

Bilbao acquired a new metro system, airport, urban motorways, railway lines and a "super port". The estuary – the backbone of the city – was cleaned and developed, financed by a water consumption tax. The industrial city switched its economic focus to technology, the service sector and tourism. At the same time, attention was dedicated to environmental friendly development. The streets of the city have seen innovative new architecture by the world's great architects, such as Norman Foster and Santiago Calatrava, making contemporary Bilbao a superb place to live, work and visit.

HISTORY LANDMARKS

1300 Bilbao founded by Diego Lopez V de Haro.

1372 Juan I of Castile increases the city's privileges.

1511 Consulate of Bilbao is created.

1521 Juan Sebastián Elcano, a Basque from Getaria, brings Magellan's round-the-world voyage home.

1704 Population of Bilbao is 5,946, having grown five-fold over a century.

1857 Banco de Bilbao founded.

1862 Railway reaches Abando station.

1874 Bilbao besieged in the Third Carlist War.

1890 Bilbao stock exchange opens.

1893 Puente de Vizcaya Transporter bridge built.

1894 Basque Nationalist Party (PNV) formed.

1900 Euskalduna shipyards founded.

1901 Banco de Bizkaia founded.

1902 The blast furnaces of the steelworks, Altos Hornos de Vizcaya, are built.

1936 Spanish Civil War begins. Bilbao is bombed by Franco's planes.

1937 Bilbao besieged from May to June. 27 April: Gernika is bombed by Franco's planes. 19 June: the Nationalists march into the city.

1939 General Franco wins the war.

1959 ETA, the Basque separatist group, founded.

1975 Death of General Franco. Accession of Juan Carlos I.

1977 First free elections in 40 years bring Socialists to power.

1979 Statute of autonomy introduced for Basque Country.

1983 Devastating floods in August kill two people.

1995 Metro inaugurated.

1996 Steelworks close.

1997 Bilbao Guggenheim Museum opens. Zubizuri bridge is built.

1999 Palacio Euskalduna palace opened.

2012 Iberdrola Tower built.

2018 Basque nationalist terrorist campaign comes to an end.

2019 Spanish general election delivers a hung parliament.

Curve of the Guggenheim

WHERE TO GO

Bilbao city centre can be best thought of as separated into two parts by the ria. Each can be explored mostly on foot. On the right (north) bank is the older section, the Casco Viejo, while the much more expansive Ensanche spreads southeastwards from the left bank. The newest architectural developments of the latter are in the area of Abandoibarra, around the Guggenheim Museum. There are a few sights beyond these two parts: across the river from the Casco Viejo and Abandoibarra respectively. Downriver, there are more sights around Portugalete and the beaches of Bilbao (reached by bus or metro).

Bilbao makes a good base for exploring the rest of the Basque Country. The north coast and San Sebastián, especially, are not to be missed and to the south are the vineyards of the Rioja wine region.

THE CASCO VIEJO

Confusingly, Bilbao has two "old towns". The city started out as a cluster of small fishing villages on the left bank, Bilbao La Vieja (Old Bilbao), and subsequently, between the 14th and 19th centuries, it was overtaken in importance by the Casco Viejo (Old Quarter), which grew across the river. Bilbao's oldest surviving

A Good Bilbo

Bilbao gets a mention in Shakespeare, in Act III, scene 5 of The Merry Wives of Windsor, Falstaff humourously compares himself to "a good bilbo", an old word for a strong but flexible kind of steel cutlass, from Bilbao, where the best Spanish sword-blades were made.

Arriaga Theatre from the Arenal Bridge

buildings are concentrated in the Casco Viejo, including many ancient mansions built on the wealth brought by international trade. It is a tight-knit labyrinth of old stone lanes, many pedestrianized, centring on the delightful arcaded main square, the Plaza Nueva. You won't need public transport here; it has to be explored on foot. The Casco Viejo is filled with bars, restaurants and chic shops and is even more lively by night than by day (especially at the weekends).

INTO THE CASCO VIEJO: PLAZA NUEVA

A good place to start exploring old Bilbao is the triangular park of the **Paseo del Arenal ❶** at the eastern end of the Puente del Arenal, the bridge which connects old and new Bilbao. Here stands the Baroque **church of San Nicolás** and the handsome Neo-Baroque **Teatro Arriaga ❷**. Subscribers who could not make it to the opening night of this theatre in 1890 listened to the inaugural opera over the telephone. The original Arriaga burnt down in 1915, however, and was rebuilt four years later. It is now used for drama and dance performances, opera and classical music (see page 87).

Calle del Correo houses some fine Baroque 18th century mansions (notably nos 8 and 14), and leads into the heart of the Casco Viejo. The first left turn off this street brings you into **Plaza Nueva ❸**, built in 1830. The 64 arcades shelter some legendary bars here, notably **Café Bilbao** and **Víctor Montes**, which are both good places for pintxos.

Off of one corner of Plaza Nueva is another square, **Plaza de Unamuno ❹**, named after the writer Miguel de Unamuno (1864–1936) who was born in Bilbao.

TWO BASQUE MUSEUMS

Two important museums stand on this square. To the north is the **Archaeology Museum** (Arkeologi Museoa; Calzadas de Mallona 2; www.euskalmuseoak.com; Tue–Sat 10am–2pm and 4–7.30pm, Sun 10.30am–2pm), set in a former train station that has been modernized to the point of being unrecognizable. Spanning three floors, the galleries cover specific eras of human history in Bizkaia, from the Neanderthals onwards, with eye-catching displays but little detail. Exhibits include a surprising number of actual skeletons, plus a fishing vessel shipwrecked during the 15th century.

On the south side of the square is the **Basque Museum** (Euskal Museoa,

Lauburu

The Lauburu or Basque cross, a symbol of Basque unity, is a common sight in the Basque Country. Four curved apostrophes are joined at their tips; the symbol dates from as far back as prehistoric times.

The Cathedral

Plaza Unamuno 4; www.euskal-museoa.eus; Mon and Wed–Fri 10am–7pm, Sat 10am–1.30pm and 4–7pm, Sun 10am–2pm; free on Thu). Devoted to Basque ethnology and history, this museum is housed in the former Colegio de San Andrés. This is a lovely retreat from the city bustle, and holds a stylized Iron Age stone figure known as the Mikeldi, depicting a hog with a disc in its belly, that is thought to have been used in ancient rituals. Displays in the museum itself trace ten thousand years of Basque fishing traditions, follow migrants as far as the western US and explain the growth of Bilbao. There's also a huge relief model of the whole of Bizkaia.

THE CATHEDRAL AND THE LIBRARY

After visiting the museums, strolling along Calle de la Cruz takes you past a Baroque church, the **Santos Juanes Church**. Fork right at the grey fountain-bench and you will find yourself on Calle de la Tendería. This is one of the so-called Siete Calles, the original seven parallel streets running down to the river, around which Bilbao was built. The other six streets are Somera, Artecalle, Belostikale, Carnicería Vieja (literally, the old butcher's – this once being the site of a slaughter house) Barrenkale and Barrenkale Barrena.

Tendería leads you to the asymmetrical porch of the **cathedral ❺** (Catedral de Santiago), a building serving as a way-station on one branch of the pilgrimage route to Santiago de Compostela in the extreme western tip of Spain. The building combines Gothic with Neo-Gothic elements and work on it has been going on more or less continuously since the end of the 14th century. The cloister is particularly worth seeing.

Calle Bidebarrieta takes you from the cathedral square to the handsome **Bidebarrieta Library ❻**, an eclectic building dating from 1890. On the way you pass a famous Casco Viejo landmark, the **Fuente del Perro** (built in 1800), in which three lions' heads spout jets of water. It's said that the name "Fountain of the Dog" was given to it because people in 19th-century Bilbao had never seen a lion, so they used a familiar animal instead.

⊙ THE SPANISH MOZART

The Baroque Spanish composer, Juan Crisóstomo Arriaga, after whom the theatre was named, was born in Bilbao in 1806 and is often described as the "Spanish Mozart" because he was a child prodigy who died young. Arriaga shared the same first two baptismal names as Mozart and the same birthday, January 27 – exactly 50 years apart. Because of his talent, his father sent him to study in Paris where he died in 1826, probably of tuberculosis, ten days before his 20th birthday and was buried in an unmarked grave in Montmartre. Arriaga's best known work, an opera, *The Happy Slaves*, written when he was 14, was premiered in Bilbao in 1826 but now survives only as fragments.

THE MARKET AND THE RIVERSIDE

Continue in the same direction as previously and you will emerge on the riverbank where you will find the **Ribera Market** ❼ (Mercado de la Ribera, Calle de la Ribera; www.mercado delaribera.net; Mon and Sat 8am–3pm, Tue–Fri 8am–2.30pm and 5–8pm).

Seven centuries since the first daily food market was established on the right bank of the Río Nervión, this permanent building remains the epicentre of life in Bilbao's old town. In its current form, it's an amalgam of a superbly elegant Art Nouveau building from 1929 with a modern revamp that has given it huge new windows, a more spacious feel and greater ease of access. Venture in to relish its vast array of fresh produce and seafood.

La Ribera Market

Adjacent to the market, next to the bridge of the same name is the **Church of San Antón** ❽ with a Renaissance façade and Baroque bell-tower. Long before the church was built (in 1546–8) there was a ford at this site which was crossed by caravans of wool coming from Castile to be loaded on ships for export. The remains of Bilbao's city wall can be seen by the altar of the church. Both church and bridge are shown on the city's official coat of arms.

Origin of Plaza de Unamuno

Miguel de Unamuno, after whom the square is named, was born at Calle de la Ronda 16, Bilbao in 1864. He was Spain's most renowned intellectual of his day but during the Civil War he came into conflict with Franco's regime. He was placed under house arrest and died in despair for his beloved Spain on 31 December 1936.

Further in the same direction is **Atxuri railway station** ❾, a 1912 building whose design has distinct influences of Basque rural architecture.

Near the station is the Plaza de la Encarnacion, named after a convent which contains a museum of religious art, **Museum of Religious Art** ❿ (Museo Diocesano de Arte Sacro; Plaza de la Encarnación 9; www.eleizmuseoa.com; open Tue–Sat 10.30am–1.30pm and 4–7pm, Sun 10.30am–1.30pm) The displays include religious plates, sculptures and paintings dating from the Romanesque period. The museum also offers the possibility of an "escape room" game (see page 97).

BILBAO LA VIEJA

Across the river from the Casco Viejo is the other old part of the city, Bilbao la Vieja, which has creativity and dynamism to offer, if not many actual sights to visit.

At the end of the Puente La Merced stands the 17th century church of the same name, that now serves a strikingly different purpose. This is now the home of **Bilborock** ⑪, a multifunctional arts space provided by the city council mainly for the staging of live music but also offering cinema, theatre, dance, installations, workshops, lectures and presentations. It can accommodate 300 people seated and 500 standing. The annual music competition of Pop-Rock Villa de Bilbao is held here in which over 30 bands compete in various categories.

The visual arts have a home in **BilbaoArte** ⑫, (Urazurrutia 32; Mon–Fri 9am–9pm), near the Puente San Antón, which has a public art gallery and many facilities for young artists including studios for painting and sculpture, engraving and screen printing workshops, digital imaging equipment, dark rooms, a film

⊙ BBVA BANK

The Banco Bilbao Vizcaya Argentaria (BBVA), one of the largest banking groups in the world, was founded in Bilbao on 28 May 1857; for a long time, its headquarters were in the Casco Viejo. Its first home was a ground-floor office on Calle Estufa but it soon moved to Calle La Ribera. In 1868 its headquarters were installed in Plazuela San Nicólas, in one of three buildings in Bilbao known familiarly as the "Edificio BBVA". The other two BBVA buildings are Gran Via 1 (on Plaza Circular, now the Torre Bizkaia) and Gran Via 12, still the central office of the bank in the city.

The bank expanded massively in the 1960s and two mergers, in 1988 and 1991, created the gigantic organization of today, with 7,844 branches in 30 countries and employing 125,749 people. Its main headquarters are now in Madrid.

set, a document centre and other rooms. As well as exhibitions it organizes courses and seminars and artist exchanges.

There is one museum worth seeking out in this corner of the city, the **Museum of Artistic Reproductions**  (Museo de Reproducciones, San Francisco, 14; www.bilboko berreginenmuseoa.eus; Tue–Sat 10am–1.30pm and 4pm–7pm, Sun 10am–2pm) which was created in 1927 to offer exact copies of masterpieces of classical art to the people of Bilbao. While you admire exact reproductions of the Elgin Marbles, works by Michelangelo, the Venus de Milo, the Winged Victory of Samothrace, the Laocoön, the Apoxyomenos, the Diana of Gabii, or the Apollo Belvedere and the Belvedere Torso.

The stairs from Plaza Unamuno

BEGOÑA AND BEYOND

If you want to escape from the clustered streets on the valley floor, you might like to climb the hillside behind the Casco Viejo for a breath of fresh air and a good view. From the Plaza Unamuno, a long broad flight of steps leads up the hillside to the massive bulk of the **Basilica de Nuestra Señora de Begoña** , a late Gothic church (started construction in 1511) which stands on the spot where the Virgin of Begoña, patroness of Bizkaia province, is said to have miraculously appeared. There's a good view over greater Bilbao from the terrace. There is a lift up to

Begoña, which is closed for repairs and should one day function again, but for now the concrete tower stands as a monument of industrial heritage.

You can continue climbing the hill beyond Begoña, where eventually you will emerge on **Monte Avril** on the Bilbao Green Ring footpath, where there are the remains of a Medieval road (between Gernika and Bilbao), dolmens and excavated trenches from the Civil War.

THE ENSANCHE

There's no way you can get lost as you explore the Ensanche, the 19th-century enlargement of Bilbao, because you will always have the city's principal artery to guide you, the long, straight,

The Abando Indalecio Prieto railway station

broad Gran Vía don Diego López de Haro that pivots on the Plaza Moyúa. The Ensanche fills the semicircle of land created by a loop of the river and the Gran via runs east to west from one old bridge, the Puente de Arenal, from the Casco Viejo to another much grander and newer bridge, the Puente Euskalduna.

Around this axis the streets – some of them wide and elegant avenues – are laid out on a geometric grid pattern. The buildings speak on them speak of mercantile wealth, civic pride and contemporary Bilbao's taste for cutting edge architecture.

AROUND THE PLAZA CIRCULAR

The Puente del Arena leads you easily from old Bilbao into the new. A few steps beyond the end of the bridge, a covered alley to your left takes you to the door of **La Sociedad Bilbaina**, a club for the well-heeled citizen which was unashamedly modelled on the clubs of London and evidence of Bilbao's long commercial relationship with the United Kingdom.

You soon reach the **Plaza Circular ⓰**. In the middle stands a statue of Diego López de Haro who founded the city of Bilbao in 1300. The square is overshadowed by the pink-and-black 88-metre high tower block, the Torre Bizkaia.

The striking metal-and-glass metro station entrances in the square are were designed by Norman Foster and have been affectionately dubbed *fosteritos* by commuters.

Not far from the square are two of Bilbao's six railway stations. One is the cheerful Art Nouveau **Santander Station** (now known as Bilbao-Concordia) which was built in 1898 and has a green and yellow façade.

The other station is the much larger mainline station of **Abando ⓰** dating from 1950. Inside, one entire wall is occupied by an enormous stained glass window depicting life and customs of the city, including Basque farmhouses, the San Antón

Café Iruña

bridge (see page 35), the Basilica de Begoña (see page 37) and references to the steel industry, fishing and sport. On one of the sides of the station is an early steam train (stationary), the Izarra, one of the first eight identical engines to run on the completed Tudela-Bilbao railway when it opened in 1863. Between the two stations is Bilbao's stock exchange (Bolsa) which opened in 1905.

From the Plaza Circular, the Gran Via sets off almost due west. Many of the city's smart shops are on or near this great artery, beginning with the **Corte Inglés** department store (see page 84). There are also plenty of bars and restaurants worth visiting.

DETOURS FROM THE GRAN VÍA

To see one of the city's best bars, however, you will need to make a detour north to the edge of the rectangular Jardines Albia. On the corner of Colón de Larreátgui and Berástegui is the **Café Iruña** ⓱ (see page 111), a Belle Epoque neo-Mudejar fantasy dating from 1903 and a hangout for the city's writers and other intellectuals. Wherever you look inside there are murals, mosaics, stained glass windows, friezes, arches, brass rails, mirrors, old adverts and a myriad other decorative details. Not far beyond the bar is the **church of Saint Vicente**

Martir. You can find your way back to the Gran Via by going via the monument to the Basque poet Antonio de Trueba (1819–1889), by the Valencian sculptor Mariano Benilliure.

There is also a good little walk on the other side of the Gran Via past Sagrado Corazon church to see the exquisite **Teatro Campos Eliseos** ⓲, which has an extraordinary Art Nouveau façade dating back to 1902.

THE GRAN VÍA EAST

Back on the Gran Via, again heading west, you will pass the eclectically ornamented façade of the **Palacio de la Diputación Foral** (no 25) ⓳, built in 1900, at the height of Bilbao's commercial and industrial prowess, as a seat for Bizkaia's provincial government.

Immediately behind it is a marvellous library; a five-storey building entirely clad in panes of glass on which are etched 173 sentences in many different languages (including Latin, Greek and Swahili). Depending on the time of day and the light conditions you will either see the writing on the outside of the library or the 300,000 volumes, freely accessible to the public, stored inside.

The mid-point of the Gran Via is marked by the elliptical **Plaza Federico**

Palacio de la Diputación Foral

Health Department Building reflections

Moyúa **20** on which stands the Carlton, the city's top hotel and the Palcio de Chavarri.

AROUND THE ALHÓNDIGA

To the south of Moyúa is Bilbao's favourite indoor playground, the **Azkuna Zentroa 21** or Alhóndiga (Plaza Arriquabar 4 ; www. azkunazentroa.eus). Entering this former wine warehouse in the new town that's popularly known as the Alhóndiga, you encounter a baffling space.

The low ceiling is supported by 43 squat Philippe Starck-designed pillars in wildly differing styles and materials, while a fiery red sun hangs in the centre.

The pillars, you will notice, are all different. The building is meant to be a melting pot of ideas and the columns symbolise an infinity of "cultures, architectures, wars and religions through which humankind has passed throughout history". A total of 120 sculptors, painters and architects worked on the columns using a variety of materials: ancient and modern: marble, brick, wood and bronze; Lecce stone and glazed terracotta; and cement and steel. They are arranged deliberately so as to enhance their variety: similar materials or echoing styles have been separated so that each column can be appreciated as it is, in its own right. The columns are intended to act as meeting points and catalysts for creativity "Behind these columns hide," says the designer Philio Starck: "they fall in love, kiss, spy and make dates…"

Elements beyond include cafés and restaurants, a basement cinema, assorted performance and exhibition spaces, and a gym. Overhead, on the top floor, is a swimming pool with a transparent glass floor.

If you want to wander further in the same direction you will come to Bilbao's **Museo Taurino ㉒** (www.plazatorosbilbao. com; Mon–Thu 10am–1.30pm, 4–6pm).

Not far from the Alhóndiga is one of the more striking pieces of new architecture in the city centre, the **Department of Health** (Alameda Recalde 3), which seems a jumble of panes of glass creating interestingly staggered reflections.

A block away, more or less in the opposite direction is the Plaza Indauxtu on which stands the **Casa de los Aldeanos ㉓**, or "painted house", a six-storey Art

The Ikurriña

The Ikurriña (or Ikurrin), the official flag of the Basque Country, which adorns many flagpoles, consists of white cross over green saltire (St Andrew's Cross) against a red background, in a similar pattern to the Union Jack flag. It was designed by nationalists in 1894 and there is no one agreed explanation for what the colours symbolise.

Nouveau block decorated with elegant murals on either side of the windows.

THE GRAN VÍA WEST

The Gran Vía continues west past the eclectic-style Edificio de Ramón de Sota (No 45). Turn off to visit the **Museo de Bellas Artes** ㉔ (Parque de Doña Casilda de Iturriza; www.museobilbao.com; Mon and Wed–Sun 10am–8pm; free after 6pm). Inevitably doomed to play second fiddle to the Guggenheim, the Bellas Artes is a high-quality art museum in its own right. Its sizeable permanent collection, housed in a bright, spacious modern annexe to its original core, ranges from anonymous medieval religious artworks to the

⊙ ATHLETIC DE BILBAO

The local first division football club, Athletic de Bilbao, has a huge following and has been highly successful since its foundation in 1898. Its selectors draw only on players from the Basque Country and those who come through the club's own youth training system.

Their home is Campo de San Mamés stadium often referred to as "La Catedral" (the Cathedral). The team is familiarly known as *los Rojiblancos* after their red-and-white-striped shirts. Another name for them is Los Leones (the Lions) after the legend of Saint Mammes (San Mamés) who was supposedly thrown to the lions by a Roman emperor but tamed the beasts and survived.

The Spanish league season runs from late August until May, and most games kick off at 5pm or 7pm on Sundays. For more information see www.athletic-club.eus.

present day. It has a sizeable collection of works by Flemish, French, Italian and Spanish painters. Highlights include El Greco's stark St Francis, Gauguin's Washerwomen in Arles and a series of landscapes by Joaquin Sorolla, many of which were painted along the Basque coast. There are also works by Velázquez, Zurbaran, Goya, Ribera and Picasso; and 20th-century artists such as Bacon and Tàpies. Basque artists such as Zuloaga, Regoyos and Echevarría are much better represented here than in the Guggenheim: look out for Anselmo Guinea's 1899 Art Nouveau panel *Back From the Pilgrimage*, and José Arrue's later depictions of idyllic village life.

In addition to its Flemish, Catalan and classical Spanish holdings, it has a modern wing with some pieces showing the influence of various international art movements on those artists who grew up under Franco, including Isabel Baquenado, Juan José Arqueretta, Andrés Nagel and Javier Morras.

Behind the museum Bilbao's largest garden the splendid **Parque de Doña Casilda de Iturrizar** ㉕ tapers towards the **Plaza Sagrado Corazón** ㉖ with a monument at the centre. Behind the 1871 **Casa de la Misericordia**, just off the square, is the **San Mamés football stadium** ㉗, home to the legendary Bilbao Athletic (see page 44).

ABANDOIBARRA

Until the mid-1990s, the area now known as Abandoibarra was as scruffy as the Ensanche was smart. Here were located the declining shipbuilding yards, railway repair sheds and transit container stores that created mass employment and generated the profits to build the bourgeois mansions of Bilbao. When such heavy industry became uncompetitive, Abandoibarra declined into a no man's land and became the redundant debris of an age that had past. For a few years it remained a sad and insalubrious waterside zone where no one in their right mind would want to hang around. Visionary planners, however, saw it otherwise. It was a blank slate, a brownfield site immediately adjacent to the city centre that

Euskalduna Shipyard and La Carola crane

invited the application of imagination. With the right level of investment and a commitment of political will the industrial remains could be swept away, and Abandoibarra transformed into the opposite of what it was before.

Now it is Bilbao's zone of luxury and leisure. It is simply a stunning example of redevelopment which stimulated the transformation of Bilbao as a whole and has become a template for what can be done to post-industrial cities around the world.

The rescue and revaluation of Abandoibarra began with the decision to site a European branch of the Guggenheim Museum here. This may be the largest and memorable piece of modern architecture in the area but there are plenty more buildings to admire. In fact, Abandoibarra has evolved into an open air exhibition of innovative buildings by diverse international architects. The soul of Abandoibarra is resolutely contemporary, in contrast to the rest of the city, but then that also means it comes without social and economic baggage and you can enjoy it without having to have a history lesson first.

MUSEO MARÍTIMO RÍA DE BILBAO

You might want to head straight for the Guggenheim but it is worth taking time to see some of the other architecture on display. To do this there is a logical route to follow from the Plaza Sagrado Corazon, at the end of the Gran Via (and at the tip of the Doña Casilda Iturrizar Park).

Traffic from the Gran Via is funnelled across the river to the neighbourhood of Deusto via the broad **Euskalduna bridge** ㉘, which opened in 1997, the same year as the Guggenheim. It is named after the shipyards that once dominated Abandoibarra. A separated, blue-roofed deck of the bridge carries wide pavements and cycle tracks and a distinctive 45-m high illumination tower rises above the bridge.

Palacio Euskalduna

Beside the bridge is the Basque Country's permanent collection of maritime items that connect it with its maritime history, **Itsasmuseum** ㉙ (Basque Maritime Museum; www.itsasmuseum.eus; Apr–Sept Tue–Sun 10am–8pm, Oct–Mar Tue–Fri 10am–6pm, Sat and Sun 10am–8pm; free on Tue). The museum explains in intricate detail exactly how the ría between the city and the sea was cleared over the centuries to deal with ever larger marine traffic. There are exhibits both inside and outside – where you can clamber aboard assorted vessels in the old docks of the shipyard outside. The emblem of the museum and the maritime history of the city is the preserved, bright red Carola crane.

A WALK THROUGH CONTEMPORARY BILBAO

On the other side of the bridge from the museum is the **Palacio Euskalduna** ㉚, a conference centre and concert hall, designed by Federico Soriano and Dolores Palacios which opened in 1999. It is an impressive edifice of glass, steel and concrete. On the third floor there is a renowned restaurant, and outside, there are various pieces of urban art.

From here, the Avenida Abandoibarra leads towards the Guggenheim, but to see more modern architecture, turn right at the Hotel Melia (by the Mexican architect Ricardo Legorreta) on

Lehendakari Leizaola. This takes you past the Zubiarte shopping centre (see page 84), designed by Robert Stern, and intended to recreate the atmosphere of a city street composed of six buildings connected by walkways. You come to the **Plaza Euzkadi**, the fulcrum of Abandoibarra, which is overlooked by César Pelli's 165-metre **Iberdrola Tower** ③ (2012), the tallest building in the Basque Country. The 25th floor can be visited at weekends (www. torreiberdrola360.com; Sat and Sun 10am–7.30pm).

On either side of the tower are housing blocks by Carlos Ferrater that are aligned parallel to the nearby Deusto Bridge. Another building of note on the Plaza Euzkadi is the **Edificio Artklass** (by Robert Krier and Marc Breitman), a block of 180 flats on 8 floors flanked by two red towers topped by different coloured domes – one green and one gold.

The Iberdrola Tower

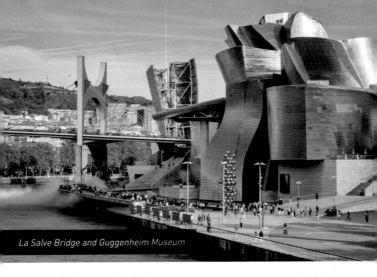

La Salve Bridge and Guggenheim Museum

Calle Ramón Rubial takes you back towards the river between two more recent buildings: Deusto University Library (by Rafael Moneo, 2009) and Bizkaia Aretoa, a university assembly hall (Alvaro Siza, 2011).

Straight on across Avenida Abandoibarra is the Pasaerala Pedro Arrupe, one of the newer pedestrian bridges across the river that has been described as "a giant dragonfly" due to its shape.

MUSEO GUGGENHEIM

Turning right on to the avenue you will see Frank Gehry's astounding **Guggenheim Museum** ❷ (www.guggenheim-bilbao.eus; July and Aug daily 10am–8pm; Sept–June Tue–Sun daily 10am–8pm) ahead of you to the east, looming over the left bank of the ria.

This is only one of the many possible ways to approach the

Guggenheim and all of them have their merits. If you have time, it is worth contemplating it from all angles.

For some people, the best way is along the river, along the quayside from the Casco Viejo; others prefer crossing the high Puente de la Salve road bridge from Deusto on the north bank.

The actual entrance, however, is on the structure's city side. You approach it from Plaza Moyua down Iparraguirre. This is the view that introduced the world to the new Guggenheim when it was used in the opening sequence of the James Bond film *The World is Not Enough* (1999).

Jeff Koons' enormous *Puppy*, clad in colourful living flowers, was originally installed as a temporary exhibit for the opening ceremony, but became a permanent fixture after Bilbainos clamoured for it to stay. Overlooking this side of the Guggenheim is the Gran Hotel Domine with an interior design by Javier Mariscal.

Completed in 1997, Bilbao's Guggenheim was hailed by the architect Philip Johnson as "the greatest building of our time". The construction of such a showpiece project on a derelict industrial site represented a colossal gamble by the Basque government, but it had the planned effect of stimulating the revitalization of Bilbao. Most people agree that this gargantuan sculpture of a building, whose sensual titanium curves glimmer like running water in the sun, is daring – but it

⊙ MASTER AND COMMANDER

Admiral Mazarredo (1745–1812) born in Bilbao is considered one of Spain's greatest naval commanders, who achieved his greatest successes against the English in the American Revolutionary War. His portrait was painted by Goya.

The Matter of Time by Richard Serra

works. However, it is perhaps inevitable that the architecture will always overshadow any artworks placed within it.

Once inside the Guggenheim, visitors flow seamlessly through the various galleries in no fixed order, crisscrossing the vast, light-filled atrium on walkways. Gehry called the largest room on the ground floor his "fish gallery"; stretching away beneath the La Salve bridge, it's permanently given over to Richard Serra's disorienting sculpture series, *The Matter of Time*, consisting of eight enormous shapes of weathered orange steel, coiled and labyrinthine.

The rest of the museum hosts top-flight temporary exhibitions, and also displays works from its own ever-growing permanent collection, including pieces by Anselm Keifer, Mark Rothko and Cy Twombly. Depending on space, you may also see selections from the Guggenheim Foundation's unparalleled holdings of contemporary art. At various points along the route it's possible to step outdoors, most notably onto the riverside terrace that holds Jeff Koons' *Tulips*.

ON FROM THE GUGGENHEIM

To continue the route of contemporary architecture, leave the museum by the exit next to the shop which will bring you onto a terrace beside the river.

Don't miss the artworks here. One of Louise Bourgeois' fearsome spindle-legged spiders, *Maman*, patrols the water's edge, while Anish Kapoor's column of glittering silver bubbles, *Tall Tree and the Eye*, stands in a reflecting pool alongside the building.

Heading east you pass underneath the Puente de la Salve, with its red arched portico, the Arcos Rojo, by the French artist Daniel Buren. The Guggenheim itself sprouts a "tower" on the far side of the bridge: a "sculptural gesture that brings the architectural design to a crescendo".

Following the broad footpath upstream you soon come to a white footbridge, the **Zubizuri** ❸, designed by Santiago Calatrava, who also designed Bilbao's airport. The base of this bridge is made of glass; arching across the river to join the Paseo Urbiarte with the Paseo Campo Volantin, many people found this slippery to walk on when it first opened, so a non-slip mat was installed.

Near the city side of the bridge there are two other contemporary buildings to admire: the **Isozaki Atea**, twin towers by the Japanese architect Arata Isozaki, that are supposed to symbolize a gateway between the Ensanche and the ria.

THE NORTH BANK

There may not be that much to see north of the river but there is a great little train ride to enjoy (especially if you have children with you). Even if you don't make it, it is still worth a stroll around the streets here. At the very least, you will get away from the crowds and start to see a bit of the "real" Bilbao.

It is a simple step to get here along the riverbank from the Arenal, on the edge of the Casco Viejo. From the Ensanche or Guggenheim, it is even easier: go straight across the Zubizuri footbridge.

CITY HALL

Bilbao's **city hall** ❸❹ stands apart from the city's other monuments at the end of Puente del Ayuntamiento (leading from Plaza Circular). It is the fourth building to bear the title since the founding of Bilbao in 1300. The first three stood on a site in the Casco Viejo, near the Puente de San Anton. Two of them were washed away by floods; the third survived but the city's administrative offices outgrew it during the early 19th century.

The site chosen for the present building was formally occupied by the Convento de San Agustin, a monastery destroyed in the First Carlist War. The present building was the work of Joaquin Rucoba, the municipal architect who also designed the Teatro Arriaga and the Alhóndiga. Its design was inspired by the public architecture of the Third Republic of France.

Bilbao's city hall

Artxanda funicular railway

Inaugurated on 17 April 1892, it is somewhat stiff and sober but reflects the pride and mercantile manner of the well-to-do Bilbainos who have always run the city. At the centre of the façade is a monumental balcony framed by eight columns and topped by a spire.

The city hall stands in the plaza Ernesto Erkoreka, a square named after the Republican mayor who led Bilbao's government when the city fell to the Nationalist forces on 19 July 1937. Erkoreka fled into exile in France but he was later handed over to Franco and imprisoned.

The 19th-century city hall is now used for mainly ceremonial functions. The city's functional administrative offices occupy a 2011 building behind it, the Edificio San Agustin.

UP ARTXANDA

Three blocks north of the river, the **Artxanda funicular railway** ㉟ (daily every 15min: June–Sept Mon–Fri 7.15am–11pm, Sat and Sun 8.15am–11pm, Oct–May Mon–Fri 7.15am–10pm, Sat and Sun 8.15am–10pm) sets off from the top of Mugica y Butrón to the summit of Arxtanda, Bilbao's rural playground. The line was built in 1915 and also serves commuters coming to and from the newer residential suburbs. Passengers are swept 770m up the mountainside in three minutes. There aren't many views along the way, but a circular park at the top offers fabulous panoramas over the city and across the verdant valley. There are picnic areas, restaurants and sports facilities at the top of Arxanda, and a hotel. There is also a shrine to visit excavated trenches from the siege of Bilbao in 1937.

If don't want to take the railway, you can catch a bus, or better still walk up one of the marked routes from La Salve bridge (next to the Guggenheim) or from the Casco Viejo via Zurbanbari.

THE UNIVERSITY AND DOWNSTREAM

Back down below and further down the river is the **University of Deusto 36**, Bilbao's first university. This building dominates the north side of the river opposite Abandoibarra and the Guggenheim, and was opened by the Society of Jesus

---

⊙ THE GREEN RING

If you feel the need to escape the noise of the city centre, or if you want good views of the metropolis, you could walk along a section of the long distance footpath that circumnavigates the surrounding hills, the Anillo Verde or Green Ring, officially designated GR228 (Gran Recorrido; long-distance footpath).

The full circuit is 38km but if you take all the variants it is possible to extend this to 64km. The route takes in four urban parks and four forest parks.

Seven signposted footpaths radiate out from the city centre to join the GR228 at various points but perhaps the easiest way point get to on to it is where it comes closest to the city centre: It is forced to cross the ria at the lowest bridging point, across the Puente de Eskalduna.

(the Jesuits) in 1886. The eclectic edifice was designed by Francisco de Cubas and it was for some time the largest structure in the city. In 1916 the university opened the first business school in the country and went on to produce politicians, economists, bankers, entrepreneurs, journalists and writers as graduates. Deusto University is still a Catholic institution that is organized around the

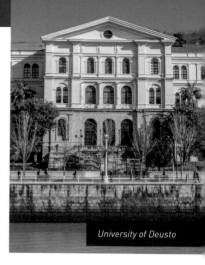

University of Deusto

motto "faith, a driver of knowledge". Only much later – long after the Civil War – was the public, secular University of the Basque Country, created with its main campus at Leioa-Erandio, north of the city.

Down the riverbank from the university (on Ribera de Botica Vieja) is a building (built in 1940), known as the **Edificio del Tigre 37** after the gigantic snarling tiger cast in concrete that adorns its corner tower.

Still heading downstream, Deusto sprouts a new elongated island, Zorrotzaurre. Described as an island for "living, working and pleasure", the peninsula-turned-island project was designed by the late Zaha Hadid and when it eventually opens, will be accessible by two bridges. The project promises to offer a new quarter that is well-connected with the rest of Bilbao, as well as providing affordable housing, cultural installations and spacious green areas.

La Passionaria

Dolores Ibarruri (1895–1989), a fiery Spanish Civil War orator known as "La Pasionaria", was born at Gallarta adjacent to Santurtzi. She is credited with the universal slogan of left-wing resistance, "No Pasaran!"("They will not pass!").

A LESSON IN BASQUE

One final sight to see on the north of the river is for the intrepid traveller willing to make a special trip to get there to learn about Basque culture. The **House of Basque** ❸❽ (Euskararen etxea/Casa de Euskera; www.azkuefundazioa.eus; Mon–Fri 9am–5pm and one Sat morning per month; free) in San Ignazio (metro line 1) is unique in the world, being an information centre explaining the origins and development of the Basque language (Euskera). The museum is designed like a train station, in which the visitor accompanies the language on its journey through time, from the first words written in Euskera in the first century AD. Guided tours are available in English.

BY THE SEA

There is a whole other side to Bilbao down on the coast, 10 kilometres downstream, where the estuary meets the Bay of Biscay. Here, there are three major attractions: an extraordinary mechanical bridge; a string of beaches; and innumerable bars and restaurants serving exquisitely fresh fish and seafood.

The port and seaside are reached from the city centre by metro line 1, that runs north of the estuary, and line 2, that runs to the south through Sestao, passing a rusting blast furnace that has been saved as a monument to Bilbao's previous industrial incarnation.

PORTUGALETE AND SANTURTZI

Just before the estuary widens into the harbour, it is straddled by a highly unusual bridge, the **Puente Bizkaia** ㊿ (Bizcaya Bridge; www.puente-colgante.com; daily 10am–7pm). It connects Las Arenas (Getxo) on the north-east bank with Portugalete on the south-west bank, via its remarkable 160-metre span. It was designed by the Basque architect-engineer, Alberto de Palacio, and constructed in 1893 in order to let the tallest ships pass without obstruction. At the time it was the first bridge in the world to carry people and traffic on a suspended gondola and was used as the model for similar bridges

Puente Bizkaia

that were erected elsewhere in Europe, Africa and the Americas – only a few of which are still in existence. Its daring employment of lightweight cables of twisted steel made it one of the outstanding achievements of the late industrial revolution.

The gondola that dangles from this transporter bridge carries passengers and vehicles across the river 24 hours a day. The walkway is open daily 10am until sunset, but far more exhilarating is to take a lift and walk across the upper beam of the bridge, 45m (150ft) above the water.

Portugalete itself is a delightful place with the old quarter, casco historico, to explore. It is built around the Gothic-Renaissance Basilica de Santa Maria and at the top of the town is the 15th-century Salazar tower. If you don't want to

⊘ CAMINO DEL NORTE

A major route of medieval pilgrimage crosses northern Spain from the French border to the shrine of Santiago de Compostela in Galicia. It is extremely popular today with long-distance walkers, cyclists and horse-riders who relish the challenge to test their capacity for perseverance.

The main route goes south of the Basque Country but there is a beautiful, less frequented variation, the Camino del Norte, along the north coast. The whole route takes 39 daily stages to get from France to Santiago; 11 of them are in the Basque Country. The Camino del Norte starts from Irun, on the border, and visits San Sebastián and Gernika before reaching Bilbao. It follows the ria to Portugalete and then continues into the neighbouring province of Cantabria. Pilgrims (whether religiously motivated or not) get a "passport" stamped at each stage of the journey as proof of their achievement.

go as far as that, the waterfront is a pleasant place to stroll along. The Neoclassical town hall, the Ayuntamiento, stands on the Plaza del Solar along with a delightful 1912 bandstand. The tourist office is also on the water-front, in a conspicuous yellow and blue building that was a former railway station known as "La Canilla". Towards the seaward end of Portugalete's waterside is a curious instrument,

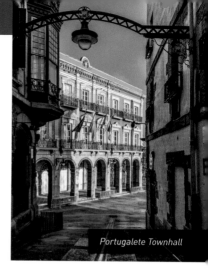

Portugalete Townhall

the Mareómetro, made in Paris in 1883 with the purpose of measuring the tides in order to know when there was enough water in the ria for it to be navigable.

Portugalete merges into **Santurtzi** ④, the port area of Bilbao, which is renowned for its sardines. Inland from Portugalete and Santurtzi is a funicular railway, less well known than that of Artxanda. This one was built 1926 to connect the mining community of La Arboleda with Trapagaran and now takes passengers up to the top station of Larreineta.

BILBAO'S BEACHES

At the other end of the Puente Bizkaia, the beaches begin. **Getxo** ④ consists of several distinct communities but centres on a pretty and lively fishing-port core, where you can dine on pintxos of fish and shellfish in old fashioned bars, al fresco-style. The town has four beaches, including the pretty

Playa de Ereaga and the more secluded Playa de Arrigunaga. There is also a small aquarium (www.getxoaquarium.com; Tue–Sun 10.30am–2pm and 4.30–8pm) on the Muelle de Arriluze seafront.

Bilbao Metro Line 1 brings day-trippers to Getxo's beaches in summer and to several other beaches around **Sopelana** and **Plentzia** ⓰. Generally, the further you are willing to travel from the city centre, the more space you will find on the sand – but remember this is the Atlantic and the water temperature is likely to be bracing...

THE BASQUE COAST

The Basque coast, north of Bilbao, is a picturesque succession of beaches, bays, cliffs, headlands, inlets, green pastures, scenic drives, and holiday resorts and fishing ports filled with bars and restaurants.

The western part – the coast of Bizkaia province – is easily accessible on day trips from Bilbao (by bus or train); alternatively you can treat a trip along the whole coast as the slow and picturesque way to drive to San Sebastián instead of taking the inland motorway.

Before you set off you will need to book ahead for a visit to the highlight of the coast, the shrine of San Juan de Gaztelugatxe.

SAN JUAN DE GAZTELUGATXE

The best place to start a drive along the north coast is **Armintza** ⓱ (reached via Plentzia), from where a corniche road leads above the cliffs to the fishing village of **Bakio** ⓲, known for its excellent beaches.

The most spectacular scenery on the coast is on the next stretch of road. **San Juan de Gaztelugatxe** is a rocky islet connected to the mainland by a causeway. If you think you have seen this place before it may because it was used as a location for *Game of Thrones*. To visit you have to request permission in advance (www.tiketa.eus/gaztelugatxe; free). At the end of the walk down a narrow path, over a stone bridge and up 241 steps is a tiny chapel dedicated to St John the Baptist. By tradition, visitors ring the chapel bell three times to bring themselves good luck and chase evil spirits away. This area around San Juan has been declared a "biotope" because it is a unique and vulnerable natural community of plants and animals.

A short way further round the coast is **Cabo Matxitxako**, a headland protruding into the Bay of Biscay. There are panoramic views from beneath the lighthouse.

San Juan de Gaztelugatxe

Elcano the Navigator

After the Portuguese navigator, Magellan, was killed in the Philippines, one of his subordinates, Juan Sebastián Elcano (a native of Getaria) completed the mission and became the first man to circumnavigate the globe.

Bermeo 45 is one of Spain's most important fishing villages, its harbour filled with brightly coloured wooden boats of all sizes and shapes crammed together in neat ranks. The Museo del Pescador (Fisherman's Museum) and the fishermen's quarter on Bermeo's Atalaya promontory are two worthwhile visits. The next stop is **Mundaka** 46, where long Atlantic rollers make it one of the best surfing spots on the coast. Mundaka stands on the Urdaibai Estuary, also known as the Ria de Gernika, where the Oka river meets the sea.

From the inlet slightly south of the port, a passenger ferry (www.urdaiferry.com; June–Sept daily every 20min) makes frequent trips across the estuary to the best beach in this area, the **Playa de Laída**, an enormous area of white sand, which at low tide stretches across the mouth of the bay in an unbroken crescent.

If you are heading eastwards along the coast, you have no choice here but to turn inland up the valley to the town of Gernika in order to cross the valley at the lowest bridging point, and then return to the coast.

GUERNIKA (GERNIKA)

Gernika 47 is the traditional heart of Basque nationalism. It was here that the Basque parliament met until 1876, and here, under the **Tree of Gernika**, that their rights were reconfirmed by successive rulers. Although the rest of the town was destroyed by the infamous **bombing** of 1937 and had to be rebuilt, the parliament, church and tree remained miraculously unscathed. For Basques, a visit to Gernika is something of a pilgrimage.

The **Casa de las Juntas** (Batzarretxea; open daily: July and Aug 10am–2pm and 4–7pm, Sept–June 10am–2pm and 4–6pm; free) is home to the parliament of Bizkaia, which was reactivated in 1979. It's not the government of the Basque Country as a whole, though – that's in Vitoria-Gasteiz. While visitors can enter the building itself, the real attraction is what's left of the **Tree of Gernika** (Gernikako Arbola), the traditional meeting place of the Basque people. Now just a stump, protected in a little columned pavilion, it stands in the adjacent grounds, close to a replacement oak planted in 2005.

Laida Beach and Pedernales Village

On a small, central open plaza, the **Gernika Peace Museum** (www.museodelapaz.org; Mar–Sept Tue–Sat 10am–7pm, Sun 10am–2pm, Oct–Feb Tue–Sat 10am–2pm & 4–6pm, Sun 10am–2pm) sets out to commemorate the town's own tragedy and explore the very concept of peace. A reconstructed living room of a typical local house enables visitors to live through the bombing raid, complete with sound effects, while an extended section honours all the victims of the Basque conflict, listed according to whether they were killed by ETA, the security forces, or other groups.

To the northeast of Gernika is the Cueva de Santimamiñe (www.santimamiñe.com; mid-Apr–mid-Oct daily, mid-Oct–mid-Apr Tue–Sun, guided tours only at fixed times). The gallery containing prehistoric wall paintings, first discovered in 1916, is closed for preservation, but the visit does include a

☉ BASQUE WHALING

From at least 1059 (probably earlier) until the 17th century, the Basques were known as the best commercial whalers in the world.

Whales were killed for their meat (that could be preserved in brine), oil (highly prized for domestic lighting) and bone (baleen) which was both strong and flexible making it perfect for corset stays.

Basque whaling began to decline when it was threatened by competition from other countries and because ships and sailors were needed by the king of Spain for his navy – not least the Armada that sailed against England in 1588. The last Basque whaling expeditions were dispatched in the mid 1750s.

3D projected virtual experience. Near the cave is the **Bosque Pintado de Oma**, a work of Land Art by Agustín Ibarrola in which tree trunks have been painted in vibrant colours.

BACK TO THE COAST

The route back to the coast takes you through the **Urdaibai Biosphere Reserve**, one of the most important wetland and bird sanctuaries in northern Spain, extending from Cabo Matxitxako across the Gernika (Guernica) estuary to Cabo Ogoño. There is a **bird observatory** ❽ at Zelaieta (www.birdcenter.org).

The first fishing village east of the Urdaibai estuary is the well-preserved **Elantxobe** ❾, with houses stacked up a steep cliff connected by a cobbled street; you'll get a superlative view of them from the top. A signposted track leads to **Mount Ogoño**, at 280m the highest cliff on the Basque coast.

As one of the coast's nicest seafront towns, the lovely old port of **Lekeitio** ❺⓿ on the west side of a broad rivermouth welcomes plenty of pleasure boats to complement its active fishing fleet. Lekeitio is blessed with a fine and very central **beach** – half beside the harbour in the heart of town, and the rest, even better, across the river to the east. The little wooded island in the middle of the bay can be reached on foot at low tide. The 15th-century **church of Santa María** features flying buttresses and a Baroque tower, and dominates Lekeitio from a high perch above the harbour. The church also contains a magnificent 16th-century Flemish Gothic altarpiece, the third largest on the peninsula after those of the cathedrals of Seville and Toledo.

Santa Catalina (Wed–Sun 11.30am–1pm and 4.30–6pm), the only lighthouse in the region that's open to the public, faces out to sea from a headland 2km north of the harbour. Inside, displays explain the history of navigation along this stretch of coast, and allow visitors to pilot a virtual "boat" between Elantxobe and Lekeitio.

The easternmost coastal town in Bizkaia, **Ondarroa** 🛈, is squeezed in on either side of the mouth of a narrow, steep-sided river. It's a workaday place, with its seaward

Lekeitio

end dominated by a no-nonsense **fishing port** filled with an eclectic set of trawlers. It has an attractive **beach** within very easy walking distance east of the harbour, and the more substantial beach of **Saturrarán** sits around the headland beyond that.

ON THE WAY TO SAN SEBASTIÁN

Zumaia 52, now in the province of Guipuzkoa, was the summer home of Ignacio Zuloaga, the best-known Basque painter of his era (1870–1945). A museum (www. espaciozuloaga.com July–Sept Wed–Fri 4–7.30pm) in his villa-studio (a former convent) displays his works, along with paintings by Zurbarán, Goya and El Greco, and sculptures by Rodin.

Getaria 53 has a long tradition of seafaring. The first man to sail around the world, **Juan Sebastián Elcano** was born in Getaria in 1487 – his ship was the only one of Magellan's fleet to make it back home. Later, Getaria became a whaling port. Now it is the centre for the production of *txakoli*, a tart young white wine made from grapes grown on the hillsides over the Atlantic.

The last resort on the coast before San Sebastián is **Zarautz** 54, which has a long stretch of a beach and also produces *txakoli*. It has a lively café life in and around its central square, making it a good place for a run on the sand, a swim in the surf and a beer on an outside terrace.

SAN SEBASTIÁN

Making the most of its glorious location, curving languidly around a magnificent semicircular bay lined with golden sand, **Donostia-San Sebastián** ⑤ ranks among the great resort cities of Europe. Although it's the capital of its region (Gipuzkoa) it has never been a major port, or much of an industrial centre. Instead, its primary identity, ever since the Spanish royal family first decamped here for the summer in 1845, has been as a summer playground. In July and August especially, it tends to be packed out, and its hotels are among the most expensive in Spain.

La Concha beach

CASCO VIEJO

Although San Sebastián's old town, or **Casco Viejo**, stands on the site where the city first developed, almost nothing predates a disastrous fire, set by British troops, in 1813. With little trace of its original walls surviving, it's a formal grid far removed from the typical old quarters of other Spanish cities. Nonetheless, it's a delight, its narrow streets and occasional pretty squares thronged in the daytime with shoppers and sightseers, and at night with revellers eager to sample its legendary pintxos bars and restaurants.

At the heart of the Casco Viejo, the **Plaza de la Constitución** makes a great arena for festivals. It even served as a bullring in the past; hence the numbers painted on the balconies. Amazingly, each window originally belonged to a separate apartment, each barely wider than a corridor; many dividing walls have now been removed, however, to make larger living spaces.

The **Museo San Telmo** (Plaza Zuloaga 1; www.santelmo museoa.com; Tue–Sun 10am–8pm), below Monte Urgull at the northeast edge of the Casco Viejo, sets out to trace the history of the Basque lands, and San Sebastián in particular. Some visitors, though, find it confusing, as it covers numerous themes and topics in a maze of buildings that incorporates a spectacular new extension. The original core, a deconsecrated convent, showcases vast monochromatic canvases by Catalan muralist Josep Maria Sert.

Go upstairs to find exhibits that cover everything from whaling to 1960 Basque pop music, by way of the regional intrigues of the Civil War; an astonishing wooden wolf trap forms the highlight of the section on rural life. Up on the top floor, the chronological displays of fine art start in the fifteenth century, and include three El Greco paintings.

Plaza de la Constitución

The Baroque facade of the **Basílica de Santa María** (31 de Agosto 46; open Mon–Sat 8am–2pm and 4–8pm; free) is visible along the slender, arrow-straight C/Mayor, the main artery of the old town, all the way from the unremarkable cathedral in the new town. You enter the main door to find that, thanks to the church's squashed-up position below Monte Urgull, the nave unexpectedly stretches not straight ahead of you but from side to side, with a huge altarpiece to your right and an alabaster Greek cross by Eduardo Chillida above the front to your left.

MONTE URGULL

San Sebastián was originally a fishing settlement at the foot of the wooded **Monte Urgull**, a steep headland that until the connecting spit was built over was virtually an island in its own right. It takes barely twenty minutes to walk around the base of the hill, along a level path that offers tremendous sunset views, or a little longer to climb to its **summit** via the trails and stairways that lead up from the Casco Viejo. Topped by a massive statue of Christ, which towers over the Castillo de la Mota, the hillside intersperses formal gardens and wilder stretches, one of which, on the far side, cradles a small **cemetery** devoted to English soldiers who died during the First Carlist War, in the 1830s.

The **Castillo de la Mota** (open late Mar– June and Sept–mid-Dec Wed–Sun 10am–5.30pm, July and Aug daily 11am–8pm) atop Monte Urgull would be worth entering simply to enjoy the magnificent views across the city and bay, but this castle also holds an enjoyable **museum**. Its entertaining romp through local history begins with the eleventh century, but focuses especially on the growth of tourism, with some great photos and film footage from the 1920s and 1930s.

Pintxos bar

Down below, the modern **aquarium** (www.aquariumss.com; Easter–June and Sept Mon–Fri 10am–8pm, Sat and Sun 10am–9pm, July and Aug daily 10am–9pm, Oct–Mar Mon–Fri 10am–7pm, Sat and Sun 10am–8pm) occupies a large concrete building on the harbour-front below Monte Urgull. A museum as much it is an aquarium, it explores the Basque relationship

Basílica de Santa María

with the sea, and even includes an entire whale skeleton. Nonetheless, it does hold tanks filled with live fish, the largest of which enables you to walk through a glass tunnel while fearsome sharks swim overhead.

PLAYA DE LA CONCHA AND MONTE IGELDO

The splendid crescent of sand that stretches all the way west from the old town to the suburb of Ondarreta, the **Playa de La Concha**, must rank among the finest city beaches in the world. If you happen to see it for the first time at high tide, you may wonder what all the fuss is about, but as the sea withdraws its full expanse is revealed. Even in the depths of winter it's usually busy with walkers and playing children, while on summer days every inch tends to be covered in tanning bodies. Swimmers escape the crowds by heading out to platforms moored offshore. Slightly further out, a little pyramidal island, the **Isla de Santa Clara**, is accessible via ferry (www.motorasdelaisla.com; Easter and June–Sept every 30min, daily 10am–8pm) that set off from near the aquarium.

The stony headland that marks an end to the seafront boulevard of the new town – most of the buildings along which, thanks to poor planning, are dull in the extreme – is topped by a former royal retreat, the **Palacio de Miramar**. The mansion itself is closed to the public, but its rolling gardens are an attractive park.

At high tide, an outcrop splits the Playa de la Concha in two; its smaller western portion therefore technically has its own name, the **Playa de Ondarreta**. At its far western end, just past the small suburb of Ondarreta, the seafront promenade finally stops amid the rocks.

The paved plaza here forms part of Eduardo Chillida's 1977 sculpture, **The Comb of the Winds** (*El Peine de los Vientos*). Two mighty iron arms claw at the waves immediately offshore, while blowholes in the plaza itself emit an eerie breathing sound most of the time, interspersed with occasional towering jets of spray.

Santa Clara Island

Peine del Viento sculpture

Forming a matching pair with Monte Urgull above the old town, the wooded hill of **Monte Igeldo** rises above the west end of the Playa de Ondarreta. Its summit can be reached via a **funicular railway** (www.monteigueldo.es; daily summer 10am–10pm, winter daily except Wed 11am–6pm; every 15min) which sets off from behind Ondarreta's beachfront tennis club. At the top you can enjoy a rather wonderful pay-per-ride amusement park, as well as tremendous views of the bay from the lookout point.

RIOJA ALAVESA

Around 90km due south of Bilbao is Spain's most famous wine growing area, Rioja, in the valley of the Ebro river. Assuming you have your own transport, exploring the picturesque villages and **bodegas** of Rioja Alavesa (the Basque part of the wine region) makes a marvellous way to spend a day.

The quickest way to get there is by the toll motorway towards Logroño, but a more picturesque approach is from Vitoria-Gasteiz (which can be visited before or after a visit to the vineyards) on the road which takes you over the Puerto de Herrera. Just past this mountain pass is a famous viewpoint, the **Balcon de la Rioja**, that offers a panorama of the plains below. This road will bring you directly to the best pick of the wine towns, lovely old **Laguardia 56** (www.laguardia-alava. com). Stretching along the crest of a low ridge overlooking the vineyards, and still surrounded by its medieval walls, it is a peaceful, tranquil spot. Within its stout gateways are slender cobbled lanes lined with ancient mansions, and connect the churches at either end. The finer of the two, Santa María de los Reyes, boasts an ornately carved Gothic doorway. Much of the town itself is actually concealed from view; the hilltop is riddled with subterranean cellars, hollowed out to store wine.

Competition between wineries is so fierce that several have invested astonishing amounts of money to attract attention. Two stand out particularly from the rest.

Framed by the hills that rise to the north, the mesmerizing **Bodegas Ysios** (tel: 902 239 773; www.ysios.com; tours Mon–Sat 11am, 1pm and 4pm, Sun 11am and 1pm; reserve online – charge includes two drinks) undulates through the vineyards 2km north of Laguardia, off the Vitoria-Gasteiz road. Its resemblance to an ancient temple is entirely deliberate; the name Ysios honours the twin Egyptian deities Isis and Osiris, and no expense was spared when architect Santiago Calatrava, also responsible for Bilbao airport and the Zubizuri footbridge, was commissioned to design a new winery. The aluminium

Vineyards in Rioja

roof surmounts a wooden structure that on a more mundane level looks like a row of wine barrels.

Just outside the appealing village of **Elciego,** 5km southwest of Laguardia, the **Bodegas Marqués de Riscal** (tel: 945 180 888; www.marquesderiscal. com; daily tours, times vary; must be reserved in advance) is among the oldest and largest of the Rioja vineyards. Several ninety-minute tours each day provide the opportunity to learn about its history, and explore every stage of manufacture, from pressing to bottling. After seeing the cellars, used to store every vintage since 1858, you also get to taste a white and a red. The *bodega* forms part of the so-called "City of Wine", the major component of which is the extraordinary hotel by Frank Gehry, creator of the Guggenheim. The tour won't take you into the hotel – for that you will have to book yourself a room – but, like the Guggenheim, it is a building to be enjoyed aesthetically mostly from the outside.

VITORIA-GASTEIZ

The capital of the Basque Country (País Vasco), as well as of the province of Araba (Alava), **Vitoria-Gasteiz** ❺❼ is a friendly old city. All the better for lying off the tourist circuit, it is well worth a couple of days' visit. Sancho el Sabio, King of Navarre, built a fortress here in 1181, on the site of the Basque village of **Gasteiz**. He renamed it **Vitoria** to celebrate his victories over Alfonso VIII of Castille, who promptly captured it back in 1200.

Stretching along a low ridge in the heart of a fertile plain, Vitoria subsequently prospered as a trading centre for wool and iron, and still boasts an unusual concentration of Renaissance palaces and fine churches. The decisive battle of the Peninsula War occurred near the city on 21 June 1813 when an allied army under Wellington defeated the retreating French forces that had previously controlled Spain.

The streets of the city's historic old town, the **Casco Medieval**, wrap themselves like a spider's web around either

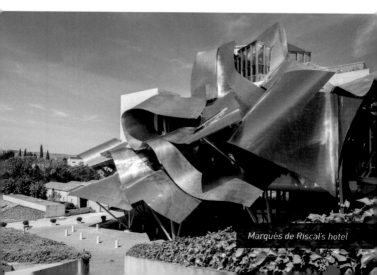

Marqués de Riscal's hotel

side of the central hill, while a neater grid of later developments, the **Ensanche**, lies below on the plain.

All Vitoria's graceful mansions and churches are built from the same greyish-gold stone, and many of the medieval buildings are amazingly well preserved. The pick of the bunch, on Calle Fray Zacarías near the cathedral, include the **Palacio de Escoriaza-Esquibel**, with its 16th-century Plateresque portal, and the **Palacio de Montehermoso**, now operating as a cultural and exhibition space. On the southern edge of the old town, **Plaza de la Virgen Blanca** is elegant, with its glassed-in balconies. If you find the hill itself a bit of a challenge, note that Vitoria offers a remarkable feature: **moving stairways** climb from both the east (Cantón de San Francisco Javier) and west (Cantón de la Soledad) sides.

Plaza de la Virgen Blanca

Work remains in progress on the **Catedral de Santa María** (www.catedral vitoria.eus; daily, hours vary; booking essential) but the building can be visited on **guided tours** which work their way up through the entire edifice, starting with displays in its ancient crypt (where there are open tombs), continuing with a hard-hat expedition high above the nave, and culminating with a light show on the superbly

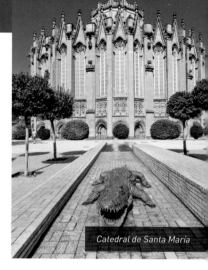

Catedral de Santa María

carved 14th-century west doorway. Some tours also include the tower and the city walls.

The **Artium** (www.artium.org; Tue–Fri 11am–2pm and 5–8pm, Sat and Sun 11am–8pm) immediately east of the old town, is an attractive museum of contemporary art. Its subterranean galleries concentrate largely on temporary exhibitions of Basque and Spanish artists, for which the Artium is able to draw on the city's permanent collection of more than three thousand works.

Another place for art lovers is the **Museo de Bellas Artes** (Tue–Fri 10am–2pm and 4–6.30pm, Sat 10am–2pm and 5–8pm, Sun 11am–2pm), housed in magnificent mansion on an attractive pedestrianized avenue in the Senda district, southwest of the centre. Its fine collection centres on the period from 1700 to 1950; highlights include *costumbrista* paintings, depicting Basque cultural and folk practices.

Old town shops

WHAT TO DO

SHOPPING

Bilbao is something close to a shopping paradise. Easy to get around on foot, it has an enormous variety of shops, both large and small, old-fashioned and ultra-modern. Whether you are looking for fashion, designer household goods or traditional souvenirs, all you need to know is where to go.

SHOPPING AREAS

Bilbao's shops can be grouped into four main areas. The mainly pedestrianized streets of the Casco Viejo have many small shops, including one specialising in traditional skills and crafts. You'll also find start up enterprises yet to make the big time, which can be good for unusual souvenirs.

Across the river, Bilbao la Vieja is an up and coming dynamic area with shops selling products from around the world, as well as designer stores, purveyors of alternative lifestyles, bookshops and art shops.

The Gran Via and its adjoining streets is characterised by upmarket brand shops dealing with fashion and accessories, jewellery, beauty products, designer goods, footwear and gourmet foodstuffs.

A new shopping district is developing around the Azkun Zentroa Alhóndiga; here you'll find bookshops, fashion retailers, florists, fancy kitchenware and household goods suppliers, giftshops and design galleries.

The resolutely modern Abandoibarra district around the Guggenheim is gaining a reputation for itself for cutting-edge modern art, as well as books, art-related gifts and pricey antiques.

Traditional beret: the txapela

No one knows where or when the flat round head-gear known as a beret was first worn but it became associated with the Basque Country during the 19th century because of its use by shepherds. Black and blue are the most typical colours but others come in red or white.

This is also the area to look for souvenir shops.

DEPARTMENT STORES AND SHOPPING CENTRES

A good one-stop shop if time is limited is Spain's ubiquitous and high quality department store, El Corte Inglés (www.elcorteingles.es; Gran Vía Don Diego López de Haro, 7-9) which sells a little of just about everything. It may not always have the widest range and you won't find many bargains, but it is reliable, the staff is generally knowledgeable and helpful and it has a no-nonsense returns policy. El Corte Inglés has a restaurant and also a decent supermarket.

The best shopping centre within easy reach of the tourist areas of Bilbao is Zubiarte in Abandoibarra (see page 49) which has over 70 shops, including many international brands, selling fashion and accessories, beauty products and services, leisure and cultural items, clothes and equipment for sport and household goods. The complex also includes a supermarket and a cinema.

WHAT TO BUY

Because of the historical British influence on the city, Bilbao is a surprisingly good place to look for upper-end gentlemen's outfitting and tailoring; check out Derby Gardeazabal (Alameda Urquijo 6). It also has something of a reputation for jewellery, such as Perodri Joyeros (at Bidebarrieta 7). Zubiri (Licenciado Poza, 33) has a long-standing reputation for its quality lingerie and corsetry. The best secondhand bookshop by far is the Libreria Astarloa (Astarloa 4) – here you will find some books in English. Or, if it is vinyl records you are after, then you will love Power Records (Villarias 5).

If you want something more traditional you might want to buy a *txapela* (Gorostiaga, Victor 9) – or Basque beret – a pair of rope-soled shoes (Bizkarguenaga, Somera 8); basket ware (Cesteria Alonso, Belostikale, 15); chocolates (Chocolates de Mendero, Licenciado Poza 16); or savoury delicacies including dried codfish (Gregorio Martin Artekale 22).

MARKETS
La Ribera (www.mercadodelaribera.biz) on the riverside of the Casco Viejo, is one of the largest permanent markets in

Sombreros Gorostiaga Hat shop

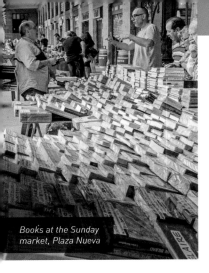

Books at the Sunday market, Plaza Nueva

Europe. It is open the mornings from Monday to Saturday, and also in the afternoons from Tuesday to Friday. Its stalls sell meat and charcuterie, fish and seafood, vegetables, frozen foods, prepared meals, conserves, cheese and bread. They are visited by the city's chefs as they compile their menus for the day according to fresh produce available in the season. There are some divine specialist stalls here – one stall specializes in pickled olives, for example, while another focuses purely on mushrooms.

Sunday is the day for outdoor markets. The best known takes place in Plaza Nueva where stalls laden with books, records, stamps and coins and collectables of all kinds appear in the arcades. Nearby there is a flower market in the Paseo del Arenal. Other Sunday markets are the flea market in Bilbao la Vieja and "Open Your Ganbara" in an old biscuit factory at Ribera de Deusto 70 in Zorrozaurre (metro: Deusto), an eclectic secondhand market with the motto, "Reduce, Reuse, Recycle".

Over 200 shopkeepers in the Casco Viejo get together twice a year to organize the "Ganja" Market to sell off their surpluses after the summer and winter seasons. Clothes, accessories, footwear, interior furnishings, household items, lingerie, crafts, gift items, sport goods, books and much more are offered at vastly reduced prices and so it is worth checking out.

ENTERTAINMENT

Modern Bilbao prides itself on being a diverse, creative and cultural city. There is almost always something going on worth seeing, especially over the summer months. The tourist information website highlights the main events but for detailed listings, including live music, see the local newspaper *El Correo* (www.elcorreo.com) or the specialist "what's on" publication, La Ria del Ocio (www.lariadelocio.es).

OPERA, CLASSICAL MUSIC, THEATRE AND CINEMA

The city's prestige venue is the **Palacio Euskalduna** (Avenida Abondoibarra, tel: 94 403 50 00; www.euskalduna.eus), an Ultramodern structure on the waterside down from the Guggenheim. It was built on the ruins of the city's last shipyard (after which it is named) and serves as home to the Bilbao Symphony Orchestra. It puts on a programme of opera and classical music, and theatrical performances.

An older venue for highbrow events, and just as renowned, is the **Teatro Arriaga** on the edge of the Casco Viejo (Plaza Arriaga; tel: 94 416 35 33; www.teatroarriaga.eus). This magnificent old-town landmark hosts dance and classical music and opera events, as well as theatrical performances.

Basque strength

During the summer months in the Basque country and especially during Bilbao's Great Week in August you will have the chance to watch competitons of unique Basque rural strength sports *Herri kirolak* including aizkolaritza (log-chopping), harrijasotzea (stone-lifting – the record stands at over 315kg), soka-tira (tug-of-war) and segalaritza (grass-cutting).

Giants and Big-Heads,
Aste Nagusia

LIVE MUSIC

The first place to look for a range of live music is **BilboRock-La** Merced (Muelle de la Merced 1; tel: 94 415 13 06; www.bilbao.net/bilborock). This large, retro-styled converted church, just across the Puente La Merced from the Casco Viejo, is among the city's best live venues for rock and alternative music.

There are plenty of other places staging live acts in all genres. Among them are **Cotton Club** (Gregorio de la Revilla 25 – note you enter on Calle Simón Bolívar; tel: 94 410 49 51; www.cottonclubbilbao.es), offering a little of everything from jazz and blues to rock and house; Kafe Antzokia (Done Bikendi 2; tel: 94 424 61 07; www.kafeantzokia.eus), a cinema-turned-nightclub which has resident DJs on Saturday nights but at other times attracts big names, from world music and reggae to folk- and punk-influenced groups and Basque musicians; and Azkena (Ibañez de Bilbao 26; tel: 94 424 08 90), a popular live music bar, with simple, minimalist decor and a dancefloor that's worth getting early there for.

NIGHTLIFE BARS AND NIGHTCLUBS

The city has a pulsating nightlife, especially at the weekends – and goes totally wild during the August fiesta, with open-air bars, live music and impromptu dancing everywhere and a truly festive atmosphere.

Bars divide broadly into two types: daytime bars and cafés (with pintxos; opening for breakfast and closing around midnight or 1am) and night-time bars, often called pubs (drinks only, sometimes with live music; these kind of bars open late,

⊙ A GREAT WEEK OF BASQUE

Bilbao's main annual celebration is the Aste Nagusia (Great Week), which starts on the first Saturday after 15th August and carries on relentlessly for the next nine consecutive days.

The weekdays during the fiesta are supposed to be working days, but most people don't try to get any serious business done. The weekends are dedicated to celebration without restraint. If you are visiting the city during these days you will have an endless, mostly free supply of entertainment. The programme of the Great Week is a heady mixture of Basque folklore, sport, music (using traditional instruments), bullfighting, bull-running in the streets and contemporary arts. There are competitions of Basque strength sports, regattas, performances of *bertsolari* (improvised musical verse in Basque tradition), and public dances in squares.

As well as all of these experiences, there are also art exhibitions and other high-brow cultural events to attend.

The whole festival is "presided" over by the figure of Marijai, the model of a plump woman in an old-fashioned dress with her arms stretched out above her head. On the last day of Aste Nagusia, Marijai is taken down to the river, placed on a boat and ceremonially burned as a symbolic way of finishing the fiesta for another year.

in the evening, and stay open until long into the small hours).

For many people a good night out involves dinner in the first kind of bar and then drinks in the second kind, or a club. You'll find both kinds of bar in the Casco Viejo. Calle Barrenkale is the heart of the frenzy. If you want somewhere more relaxing, the beautiful Plaza Nueva is a better choice. The Ensanche, too, has plenty of pubs and bars. Trends change and if you want to find the nightspot of the moment, the best bet is to follow the crowds.

SPORTS AND ACTIVITIES PLAN

If you need a break from visiting historical and cultural landmarks, Bilbao (and the Basque Country) offers a range of sports and activities that you can participate in, from the gentle-paced to the adrenaline-filled. You might also like to attend a sporting event as a spectator to get a better understanding of the Bilbaino way of life.

CYCLING AND OTHER WHEELS

The entire city centre (Casco Viejo, Ensanche, and Abandoibarra), and the river valley downstream, is flat, making it easy to get around by bike. To the north, south and east, the hills close in on the city and you might have to get off and push on the outward journey but the return will be a breeze. Outside the city, there aren't many quiet, traffic-free backroads, meaning that you will have to use main roads.

There are many dedicated cycle tracks in the city, but when using them take care around aimlessly wandering pedestrians who may have right of way.

You can hire bikes from several shops (such as www.bilbao biketours.com) for the day. You can also rent tandems, four-wheel pedal-carts, roller skates and even hoverboards.

River cruise in Bilbao

RIVER CRUISING

Bilbaobentura (www.bilobentura.com) near the Maritime Museum will rent you a canoe to paddle up and down the river, but there's a limit to how far you can go. River Cheer (www.rivercheer.com) provide self-operated motorboats and give you instructions on how to use it. If you don't want to do the work yourself, El Bote (www.elbote.com) offers hop-on-hop-off river cruises that go all the way down to Portugalete and the transporter bridge (see page 60).

HIKING

The Basque Country has some superb countryside and the green hills around Bilbao are within easy reach of the city centre. The Bilbao Green Ring even goes through the urban area. Another possibility is to walk a section of the popular Camino de Santiago pilgrimage route, such as the Camino

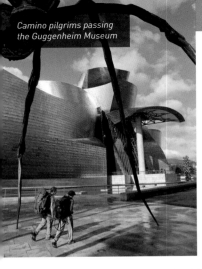
Camino pilgrims passing the Guggenheim Museum

Francés (the French way), Camino Portugués (the Portuguese way) or the Camino Primitivo (the original way).

WATERSPORTS

The nearest beaches of the Basque Coast (see page 62) can be quickly reached from Bilbao by Metro Line 1 which terminates in Plentzia. They are good for all watersports including sailing and scuba diving but given this is the Atlantic Ocean you will need a full wetsuit. Mundaka (see page 64) is a legendary surfers' destination; the surfing season runs roughly from September to April. If you prefer tamer swimming, the iconic Azkuna Zentroa has a swimming pool upstairs, as well as a fitness centre.

ADVENTURE SPORTS

You'll have to go out of the city for thrilling outdoor activities, bar one exception. By arrangement you can climb the girders of the Bizkaia Bridge with ropes and abseil down from the top (37m).

GOLF

There are five golf courses within easy reach of Bilbao: Uraburu, Palacio de Urgoiti, Club de Campo Laukariz, Real Sociedad de Golf de Neguri and Meaztegi. For information see www.1golf.eu/en/golf-courses/spain/cities/bilbao.

WHALE WATCHING

Verballenas (www.verballenas.com) takes passengers on guided trips into the Gulf of Bizkaia for a chance to see whales and sea birds. They depart on certain days (depending on the weather) from July to August from Santurzi and Bermeo. The trip takes 8–9 hours and covers 80 nautical miles. The day before departure you are invited to attend a seminar explaining the fauna you are likely to see.

SPECTATOR SPORTS

Bilbao's – and Spain's favourite spectator sport by far – is soccer. Support for the local team, Athletic Bilbao (see page 44), verges on adoration. Second in popularity is *pelota vasca*

⊙ A TRADITIONAL GAME OF PELOTA VASCA

A favourite traditional sport in Bilbao is *pelota vasca*, a ball game which is played against a high wall, a little like squash.

There are several variations of *pelota* but the most spectacular is *cesta punta* (known as *jai alai* outside Spain). This is played in long court (called a *fronton*) and at high velocity using a leather and wicker scoop-shaped glove called a *xistera*. There are singles and doubles versions and it is said to be the fastest game in the world. Other forms of *pelota* use a bat or a bare hand.

Almost every town in the Basque Country has its *fronton* for impromptu games between friends and neighbours; this was originally (and is still often the case) the wall of a church.

The largest *fronton* in the Basque Country is the Frontón Bizkaia in Miribilla, adjacent to Bilbao la Vieja. There is also a renowned court in Gernika.

(Basque Pelota), where various ball games are played against a wall (or *fronton*) – similar to squash. Other sporting events you will see advertised are basketball (see www.acb.com for details of the national league), regattas and, during the Great Week in August, traditional Basque sports of strength and stamina.

BULLFIGHTING

Considered something between a sport and an art, bullfighting still takes place in Bilbao's Plaza de Toros although there are increasing ethical objections to it. There are nine consecutive afternoons of bullfights during the Great Week in August. It is best to go with someone who knows how the *corrida* is orchestrated, or at least read up on it so you have all the information you need to know beforehand.

ACTIVITIES FOR CHILDREN

Spain is a fabulous country to travel with children of any age; they will be well received everywhere, and babies and toddlers, in particular, will be the centre of attention.

You will probably have to change your usual routine, since young children stay up late in Spain, especially in the summer. It's very

Basque wood chopping competition

common for them to be running around pavement cafés and public squares after 10pm or 11pm, and yours will no doubt enjoy joining in.

All that said, they may not want to be dragged around the same sights as you want to visit and the best bet is to interweave some child-friendly activities into your schedule. Here are some ideas.

TRANSPORT

Getting around can be fun in itself. The metro and tram are both simple to use. A boat trip down the river (see page 91) is always entertaining and the Artxanda funicular allows you to get out of the city for a while. For full autonomy you could hire bikes (see page 90) or canoes (see page 91).

MUSEUMS AND OTHER SIGHTS

Children are more likely to respond to art if you let them experience it in their own way and at their own pace. The modern art of the Guggenheim (see page 50) – both inside and outside – can be appealing to children, and rather than trying to see everything, it is better to focus on a particular section of the collection. The Museo de Bellas Artes (see page 81) offers an audio guide especially for children, telling ten stories about ten chosen works of art. The Maritime Museum (see page 48; partly open air) and the Basque Museum (see page 31) are both child-friendly and full of interesting objects.

PARKS AND OTHER SPACES TO RUN AROUND

Bilbao has many parks to run around in. The best one for children is the Doña Casilda Iturrizar (see page 45). Located next to the Museum of Fire Arts, it features playgrounds,

Ride at Monte Igeldo's amusement park

an ice cream stall and a duck pond. There are also green spaces between the Guggenheim and Palacio Euskalduna. Indeed, all the riverbanks (north and south) are lively places to be when the weather is good. The Parque Etxebarria is an immense open space within walking distance of the Casco Viejo, and the Parque Miribilla is adjacent to the streets of Bilbao La Vieja.

BILBAO'S SEASIDE

Bilbao's beaches are only a short metro ride down line 1. A morning's sightseeing can be rewarded with an afternoon on the beach.

Crossing the Bizkaia Bridge (see page 59) by the high-level walkway is an impressive experience for any age. It is also fun to ride across the river in the gondola. Getxo, on the north side of the bridge, has an aquarium (see page 62). To really make the most of a day at the seaside, you could start with a boat trip to Portugalate (see page 59).

ESCAPE ROOMS

Escape Room games have become increasingly popular in Bilbao. The city has six game installations in which teams of 2–6 players are placed in a room and have to solve a puzzle and within 60 minutes to "escape". They are mainly intended for adults but teenagers will enjoy them just as much. Some have a lower age limit and all insist that there must be at least one adult in a team if it includes one or more people under 16. The six are:

Mad Mansion (www.madmansion.es; escape rooms in Bilbao and Santurzi; minimum age 10)

Igarkizun (www.igarkizun.com; no lower age limit)

El Sótano Juegos (www.elsotaniojuegos.es; based on the theme of Alice in Wonderland)

Guarida Aventura (www.guaridaaventura.com)

Bilbaout (www.bilbaout.com; minimum age 12)

Atxuri Abbey (www.abadiadeatxuri.com; the game is combined with a visit to the Muse del Arte Sacro – see page 35. It is mainly intended for adults; minimum age 11)

DAY TRIPS

Beyond the city, the north coast (especially San Juan de Gaztelugatxe; see page 62) makes a great day out. Another worthwhile excursion is to the Cueva de Santimamiñe (see page 66) near Gernika, which can be combined with a tree-spotting trek through the Bosque Pintado de Oma (see page 67). Any child who loves wildlife will enjoy the Urdaibai bird center (see page 67), downriver from Gernika. As well as a sensational beach, San Sebastián has a renowned aquarium (see page 73) and an amusement park that can be reached by funicular up to Monte Igeldo.

FIESTAS

There is usually something going on somewhere in the city. Children will love the street theatre festival in early July and the innumerable entertainments of the Great Week in last half of August.

CALENDAR OF EVENTS

January 5: Parade of the Three Kings. From the Plaza Moyúa via the Gran Vía and Plaza Circular to the City Hall. In Spain, children get their presents from the Kings – not Father Christmas.

Jan (last week): Start of Danza Plazetan, a festival of traditional Basque dance in the streets and squares that continues all year.

February 3: Day of Saint Blaise (San Blas). People congregate in around the church of San Nicolas to buy traditional rosquillas (ring-shaped pastries) and marshmallow sweets from street stalls.

February 5: Day of St Agatha (Santa Agueda). Impromptu choirs sing from door to door while marking the rhythm by banging a wooden staff or *makila* on the ground.

Feb/Mar: (Weekend before Ash Wednesday; date varies according to Easter). Carnival (Carneval). Celebrations centre on two traditional characters, Farolin and Zarambolas, and end with the burlesque ritual, "the burning of the sardine".

Mar/Apr: Easter Week (Semana Santa): Easter Sunday is also Aberri Eguna, the unofficial Basque National Day, with a celebration of Basque Culture and nationalism.

July (first week): Kalealdia Street Theatre Festival in the Parque Doña Cassilda Iturrizar, Gran Via and Casco Viejo.

August 15: Aste Nagusia/Semana Grande (Great Week). The city's principal fiesta. Also: El Amatxu; thousands of Pilgrims converge on the Basilica de Begoña, some having walked all night.

September (last weekend): Open House in Bilbao, Barakaldo and Gexto. Two days during which public and private buildings open their doors to the public.

October 11: Dia del Virgen de Begoña. A second mass pilgrimage.

October/November: Pop-Rock Villa de Bilbao popular music competition.

November 25: Euskadi Eguna. The official Basque country holiday.

December 23: Olentzero parade. Plaza de Moyua to the Teatro Arriaga. A character from Basque folklore comes down from the mountains bringing gifts for the children.

EATING OUT

Second to none in Spain, Basque cuisine can stand comparison to the best in Europe. Fishermen's kitchens, country farmsteads, gourmet tapas bars and star chefs set standards across the board from market bars to haute cuisine. This is the place to splash out on eating well.

While not quite on a par with San Sebastián – the star turn of Basque cuisine – Bilbao is not far behind and still ranks among the culinary capitals of Spain. Innovative **restaurants** and Michelin-star winners knock out everything from traditional Basque favourites to high-class *nueva cocina vasca* meals.

In the best restaurant, a meal (without wine) can cost as much as a modest hotel room for the night, but there are plenty of more humble restaurants where you will eat well for a reasonable price.

If you don't want to sit down for a more formal service, you can still enjoy stunning Basque cuisine standing at the bar by browsing through the displays of pintxos (tapas). Taking a high-speed *txikitear* (bar-to-bar pintxos crawl) through the Casco Viejo of Bilbao is an essential part of any visit – the best targets tend to be clustered in the *siete calles* (seven streets), bordered by Ronda and Pelota, but Calle de la Diputación in the Ensanche also holds good options. San Sebastián's old town is also a gourmet's paradise.

Wherever you stop to eat, what will strike you the most

Txakoli

Bilbao's favourite white wine is the slightly sparkling *txakoli*, which is often drunk as an aperitif with pintxos. It is homegrown on the Basque coast around the town of Getaria.

is the sheer variety of what is on offer. The best ingredients from all over Spain make their way here: Atlantic fish and shellfish; game and shepherds' cheeses from the mountains; asparagus and artichokes from market gardens; prime cuts of beef and ham – you want it, you will find it somewhere prepared with finesse.

EATING HOURS

Spanish people in general eat later than their European neighbours. Many of them have a light breakfast and a mini-meal half way through the morning (around 10.30 or 11am). Most restaurants won't open until 1.30pm and will serve meals until about 3.30pm.

Dinner is proverbially late (9pm to 10.30pm is typical) but you can always have merienda – an afternoon snack at a pastelería or café at about 6 or 7pm.

Things are changing, however, and a big city like Bilbao has the usual fast food chains which are open from early until late without closing. In touristy areas, restaurants and hotel dining rooms are also used to serving meals earlier than usual to suit their clientele.

At any time of day there are pintxos to provide a snack or comprise an impromptu full meal. If you want more than a morsel to go with a drink, order a ración (a full plate).

Anchovies

WHERE TO EAT

Top restaurants may aim to serve haute cuisine but for authentic food you can't do better than where the locals eat and order what they have. There are plenty of places to eat which may not look like anything special from the outside but which serve hearty, healthy homemade dishes based on good raw ingredients, washed down with a glass or two of the local wine. Whether or not there is a menu in the bar or restaurant you find yourself in, don't be afraid to tell a waiter exactly what you want: usually he or she, and the rest of the staff, will be happy to oblige.

Places which serve food go by a variety of names other than restaurante. Mesón, posada and tasca are all old words for an "inn". The speciality of an asador is roasting meat and a marisquería will have little else on the menu except seafood. The simplest restaurant will style itself as a casa de comidas, a "a place to eat". Almost every bar will serve something to eat: sandwiches and tapas at least, but it may well have a dining room (comedor) attached.

MENUS

In Spanish, menú is not the written list of everything available to eat, but a set menu offering a limited range of options. The menu is la carta.

Every restaurant in Spain offers a three-course menú del día on weekday lunchtimes, which is often extremely good value. Usually the price and details are marked up on the street outside. A pitcher of house wine and coffee may be included. In the simplest restaurant there will be no written menu: your breathless waiter will reel off the choices and you'll have to decide on the spot. Don't be intimidated: ask him to repeat or explain anything you didn't catch. A menú de degustación is

An array of delicious pintxos

something entirely different: a sampler menu of the best the restaurant has to offer, usually at a fairly steep price.

FISH AND SEAFOOD

To say that the Basques love fish and seafood would be an understatement. Their cuisine – both traditional and most modern varieties – depends on the catches from the fishing ports of the north coast.

Two species of fish in particular appear on almost all menus. Hake (*merluza*) is a ubiquitous staple. One signature dish made with it is *kokotxas*: gullet of hake (tender flesh from the throat).

Even more common is cod (*bacalao*) which is often used in its dry salted form and appears in a variety of dishes such as *bacalo al pil-pil* and *bacalao a la vizcaina*.

Basque chefs also make great use of sardines (*sardinas*), from Santurtzi (see page 61) and anchovies (*anchoas*) which can be served fresh or preserved as *boquerones* – marinated in vinegar and oil as a tapa.

Other fish you may come across in restaurants are bonito (white tuna, usually grilled, monkfish (rape), sea bream (*besugo*) and tuna (*atún* or *bonito*), swordfish (pez espada).

Seafood comes in a similar abundance and it may well have been landed a few hours before you eat it. Note that fish and seafood is sometimes priced on the menu by weight, so what appears to be an inexpensive dish may prove very costly.

VEGETARIANS AND VEGAN CUISINE

Spain is a proudly meat- and fish- eating country and only in the largest cities, Bilbao and San Sebastián, will you find specifically vegetarian and vegan restaurants – although many

⊘ PINTXOS

No one in Spain drinks on an empty stomach. Having a drink with friends is the opportunity to eat something tasty. On the counter top of every bar in the land there is something to eat to accompany your glass of wine or beer. In the Basque Country the art of the tapa or pintxo is elevated to excellence.

A pinxto can be almost anything tasty and it usually consists of one or two ingredients skewered with a cocktail stick and fixed to a slice of baguette. Some pintxos in which the ingredient can't be skewered, or which come with a sauce, are served on a small plate instead.

Pintxos can be eaten standing up or sitting down. They are ordered and paid for separate to drinks. Point to what you want to eat on the bar and settle up at the end. If in doubt, count the number of cocktail sticks in front of you.

Waitress serving Txakoli

restaurants now style themselves as "vegetarian friendly". It is increasingly common to see menus marked up with a variety of symbols indicating whether a dish complies with certain dietary requirements. Bar and restaurant staff will generally do what they can for you; even the tiniest place with rustle up something simple to order if you explain the situation, even if it is only a salad or tortilla de patata. They may leave out an ingredient or bump up a meat-free starter or side dish into a main course if requested, or provide something that is not on the menu.

COLD DRINKS

One of the great pleasures of eating out in Spain is the chance to sample some of the country's excellent wines. At lunchtime, a glass or small pitcher of the house wine – often served straight from the barrel – may be included in the *menú del día*. In recent years Spanish wine has enjoyed a renaissance, led largely by the international success of famous wine-producing regions like La Rioja, where most of Bilbao's red wine comes from. Other regions – not perhaps so well-known abroad – are also well worth investigating. For white wine, you may want to try *txakoli*, which is produced on the coast (see page 69).

Beer (*cerveza*) is nearly always lager, though some Spanish breweries also now make stout-style brews, wheat beers and other types. It comes in 300ml bottles (*botellines*) or, for about the same price, on tap – a caña of draught beer is a small glass and asking for un tubo (a tubular glass) gets you about half a pint. A shandy is a clara, either with fizzy lemon (*con limón*) or lemonade (*con casera* or *con blanca*). In San Sebastián, cider is also a popular drink.

Every bar serves a vast range of Spanish-spirits and you will often be served a quantity at the barista's discretion rather than a measured amount. Even early in the morning, you are welcome to ask for a shot of coñac (brandy) to put into your

◎ RIOJA WINE

Spain's most famous red wines are produced in the Rioja region around the valley of the Ebro river.

Until the late 19th century, Spain's wines were by and large locally produced and were not distributed. But in 1860, two marquises, exiled in Bordeaux, returned to their native Rioja heady with the notion that they might emulate the great Bordeaux wines by ageing the Rioja wines in oak barrels. This they did and the houses of the Marqués de Riscal and Marqués de Murrieta, still active today, gave Spanish wines their first reputation abroad.

There are 350 wine makers in the Rioja region, which covers more than 500 sq km (200 sq miles). It stretches alongside the Ebro river and is divided into three areas: La Rioja Baja in the east, where the main town is Calahorra; La Rioja Alta, which includes Haro and Logroño (the main wine towns for the region); and, to the north, La Rioja Alavesa in the Basque Country.

coffee. At the end of a meal you may be offered a chupito – a little shot glass of flavoured schnapps or local firewater. In the Basque Country, this is often *patxarán* (sloe gin). A popular drink for a night out is a Cuba Libre (rum and Coke).

You can safely drink the water in Bilbao but if you want a bottle of mineral water ask for agua mineral con gas for sparkling or *sin gas* (still).

HOT DRINKS

Café (coffee) is invariably an espresso (café solo); for a large cup of weaker, black coffee, ask for an americano. A café cortado is a café solo with a drop of milk; a café con leche is made with lots of hot milk. Spaniards almost only drink this kind of coffee at breakfast time and you'll get strange looks if you

Historic restaurant Victor Montes on Plaza Nueva

order it at any other time of the day unless you're in a tourist hotspot. Coffee is also frequently mixed with brandy, cognac or whisky, all such concoctions being called *carajillo*. Iced coffee is café con hielo. Chocolate (hot chocolate) is a popular breakfast drink, or for after a long night on the town. It's usually thick and rich, so for a thinner, cocoa-style drink, ask for a brand name, like Cola Cao.

Spaniards usually drink té (tea) black, so if you want milk it's safest to ask for it afterwards, since ordering té con leche might well get you a glass of warm milk with a tea bag floating on top. Herbal teas (infusions) are widely available, like manzanilla (camomile), poleo (mint tea) and hierba luisa (lemon verbena).

TO HELP YOU ORDER

Could we have a table for two/four **Una mesa para dos/ cuatro personas, por favor**

Waiter, please! **Camarero, por favor**

Could I see the menu please? **¿Me enseña el menu, por favor?**

I'd like a/an/some... **Me gustaría un/un poco de**

I am a vegetarian **Soy vegetariano**

I am on a diet **Estoy a régimen**

What do you recommend? **¿Qué recomienda?**

Do you have local specialities? **¿Hay especialidades locales?**

I'd like to order **Quiero pedir**

That is not what I ordered **Ésto no es lo que he pedido**

May I have more bread/wine? **¿Me trae más pan/vino?**

The bill, please **La cuenta, por favor**

Enjoy your meal **Buen provecho** (A customary salutation when someone else is eating).

USEFUL WORDS

Fork **tenedor**
Knife **cuchillo**
Spoon **cuchara**
Plate **plato**
Glass **vaso**

Wine glass **copa**
Napkin **servilleta**
Bread **pan**
Salt **sal**

TO READ THE MENU

Marmitako Basque fish dish

Menestra mixed vegetables dish

Ensalada salad

Tortilla omelette. The classic tortilla española is made
with potatoes

Bacalao cod that may be served *a la vizcaina* or *al pil-pil*

Txangurro spider crab

Pintxos tapas

Alubias de tolosa red beans

Merluza hake

Txipirones (or calamares) en su tinta squid cooked in
its ink

Gambas, langostinos and cigalas large juicy prawns

Langosta lobster

Boquerones fresh anchovies

Chanquetes whitebait (usually tossed in flour and deep-
fried whole)

Pez espada swordfish

Mero sea bass

Bonito tuna

Rape monkfish

Besugo sea bream

Pisto mixed vegetables in a tomato sauce

PLACES TO EAT

Eating out in Bilbao is a great pleasure for any visit. Best of all, you have plenty of choice, whatever your taste and budget. Dining in the Basque Country varies from the phenomenally expensive (famous gourmet restaurants serving elegant haute cuisine) to the inexpensive (neighbourhood bars serving tapas and *raciónes*), with local, traditional and international options. A service charge may or may not be included in your bill; there's no standard amount to tip in Spain, but it's customary to round the amount up to the nearest 5 or 10 euros.

€€€	over 40 euros
€€	20–40 euros
€	under 20 euros

CASCO VIEJO

Berton €–€€ *Jardines 11, tel: 94 416 70 35, www.berton.eus*. This friendly Casco Viejo bar, a warm, inviting space with some outside tables and lots of drinking space inside, has been such a success that it now has three neighbouring offshoots, including a recommended restaurant. It offers fresh modern pintxos, including quails' eggs with prawns and mushrooms, and lots of ham options, plus *raciónes* of prawns, anchovies and the like. Closed Mon.

Café Bar €€ *Bilbao Plaza Nueva 6, tel: 94 415 16 71, www.bilbao-cafebar.com*. Exceptional anchovy, ham and *bacalao al pil-pil* pintxos, served by *simpático* staff, with everything labelled on the counter in the stylish old blue-tiled café interior, and some tables on the Casco Viejo's lovely main square.

Café Bizuete € *Plaza Santiago 6b, tel: 944 794 278*. The most pleasant spot for coffee in the Casco Viejo, this old-fashioned café faces the cathedral across a small square, with plenty of outdoor tables. Breakfast is served until noon, with pintxos and sandwiches available later on; most locals, however, simply drop in for coffee and a cake.

Los Fueros €€€ *Fueros 6, tel: 94 415 30 47, www.losfueros.com.* Tucked in behind the back of Plaza Nueva, this small restaurant offers an escape from the usual old-town crowds. Order *raciónes* such as their signature grilled prawns à la carte or give yourself a real treat with a set menu.

Gure Toki €€ *Plaza Nueva 12, tel: 94 415 80 37, www.guretoki.com.* Snuggled into the corner of the Casco Viejo's main square, this recently expanded tapas bar offers irresistible, eye-catching pintxos *ornamentales* including lovely langoustine and squid concoctions. You can also buy a more substantial salad to eat at the barrels out on the square itself.

Gatz € *Santa María 10, tel: 94 415 48 61, www.bargatz.com.* Cosy late-night tapas bar in the old town, its blue walls festooned with vintage photos, where a mixed younger crowd enjoys exquisite pintxos such as delicious cod, or the Basque equivalent of ratatouille in a tiny tart. Good selection of wines and beers.

Irrintzi € *Santa María 8, tel: 94 416 76 16, www.irrintzi.es.* Hip, buzzing old-town tapas bar, with groovy murals plus some of Bilbao's most creative pintxos, such as a monkfish lollipop served with strawberry gazpacho in a glass, or roast beef with spinach mousse.

Mandoya €€ *Perro 3–5, tel: 94 415 02 28, www.restaurantemandoya.com.* Classical and modern Basque cuisine. A cut above the average lunch-time restaurant (it only opens in the evenings on Fridays and Saturdays) with exquisite dishes made from locally sourced ingredients; lobster is a speciality. If in doubt, try the taster or deli menu. Vegetarian and gluten free options available. Closed Mon.

Xukela €€ *El Perro 2, tel: 94 415 97 72, www.xukela.com.* With its red panelling and checked linens, this perennially popular Casco Viejo tapas bar is oddly reminiscent of a French bistro, and serves substantial enough *raciónes* to make a hearty meal; but it's best known for its wide range of snacks and top-class wine list. There's plenty of open space for drinkers who prefer to stand.

Río Oja €€€ *El Perro 6, tel: 94 415 08 71,* www.rio-oja.com. Cosy, old-fashioned, much-loved and exceptionally inexpensive Casco Viejo restaurant with an unusual emphasis on hearty stews (*cazuelas*) and sauces, arrayed along the bar for diners' inspection. With clams in green sauce, or quail stew, this is a place to experiment a little; they also serve *raciónes*. Closed Mon.

Victor Montes €€ *Plaza Nueva 8, tel: 94 415 70 67,* www.victormontes. com. Atmospheric bar and dining room, lined with a collection of over 1600 wines, on the attractive main square of the old town. Traditional grills, special hams and fresh fish are served in the main, very popular dining room, and sumptuous pintxos in the bar; in summer they put out tables on the square.

ENSANCHE

Bascook €€€ *Barroeta Aldamar 8, tel: 94 400 99 77,* www.bascook.com. Among the most popular recent additions to Bilbao's dining scene, *Bascook* is the brainchild of chef Aitor Elizegi. His playful ideas include having a menu that's also a magazine, and offering three separate cuisines – world, vegetarian and, for those with time to linger, slow food. A set menu is available at lunchtime and another, pricier one in the evening.

Café Iruña €€ *Colón de Larreategui, tel: 94 423 70 21,* www.grupoiruna. net. Historic café and bar established in 1903, facing the petite Jardines de Albia park. Elaborate murals, ornate Mudéjar decor and traditional grocery-style tiling form its three sections – a bar, a café and a dining room – marvellously atmospheric. It's busy around breakfast time; later on it serves a set dinner menu, and it's also a great spot for a drink or a few pintxos – the *pinchos morunos*, or mini-kebabs, are especially worth trying.

Garibolo € *Fernandez del Campo Kalea 7, tel: 94 422 32 55*, www.garibolo. com. A vegetarian menu south of the Gran Via behind Abando station. Good selection of salads, soups and fat-free dishes. It offers a large choice of homemade puddings and a cellar of organic wines.

El Globo € *Diputación 8, tel: 94 415 42 21*, www.barelglobo.es. Creative, high-quality pintxos near Plaza Moyúa in the central Abando district. The interior decor is part wine bar, part upscale sandwich bar, and there's also outdoor seating – order through the hatch in the wall. Plentiful seafood options include baby squid with caramelized onions, or you can opt for goat's cheese. Closed Sun.

ABANDOIBARRA

Atea €€ *Paseo de Uribitarte 4, tel: 94 400 58 69*, www.atearestaurante. com. Good-value, central restaurant south of the river near the Zubizuri footbridge, where the modern dining room lurks behind the facade of a former customs warehouse. There are also outdoor tables. With the emphasis on a quick turnaround, the set lunch is a tray holding three pintxos plus main course, salad and dessert. Closed Mon.

Bistro Guggenheim €€–€€€ *Guggenheim Museum, tel: 94 423 93 33*, www.bistroguggenheimbilbao.com. The Guggenheim's in-house bistro serves a great-value set lunch menu of zestful modern Basque cuisine, and choice of dinner menus, while its café and terrace bar sell simpler snacks all day, including pintxos and salads.

Copper Deli € *Mazarredo 6 and Plaza del Museo 3, tel: 94 657 08 99*, www. copperdeli.com Two fast food restaurants styled on a New York deli. It aims to offer quick, simple and healthy vegetarian, vegan and gluten-free meals.

Etxanobe Euskalduna €€€ *Avda. Abandoibarra, 4 tel: 94 442 10 71*, www.en.etxanobe.com. Enjoying tremendous views of the city from its open-air terrace, the Michelin-starred *Etxanobe* is run by celebrated Basque chef Fernando Canales. Innovative, contemporary cuisine, but at a hefty price.

SANTURTZI

Mandanga Hogar del Pescador €€ *Puerto Pesquero, tel: 94 461 02 11,* www.hogardelpescadorsanturce.es In the harbour area of Santurtzi, a 20-minute walk from Portugalete, is the quayside restaurant terrace with views that is locally famous for its besugo (sea bream) and fresh grilled sardines.

BASQUE COAST

Mentrame € *Portu 2, Elantxobe, tel: 94 673 92 50.* Simple bar, down by the port, with a decent selection of pintxos and some more substantial *raciónes*.

Politena € *Nagusia 9, Getaria, tel: 94 314 01 13.* Like several bars along Getaria's very pretty principal lane, this friendly spot sets out pintxos on the bar and serves full meals in a dining room further back, and also has a couple of outdoor tables. Much better value than you'll find along the seafront.

Oskarbi € *Muelle Txatxo Kaia 2. Lekeitio, tel: 94 624 38 59.* The pick of several similar restaurants along the waterfront, serving good-value meals on its large canopied terrace. The lunch menu includes salad or a hearty soup, a whole grilled fish, dessert and wine.

Los Txopos €€ *Devnaren 4, Mundaka, tel: 94 687 64 82.* Tapas bar with a full menu of *raciónes*. The seafront location and expansive terrace seating are the attraction more than the quality of the food.

GERNIKA

Baserri Maitea €€€ *Atzondoa, Forua tel: 94 625 34 08,* www.baserri maitea.com. Whether you eat in the spacious dining room inside this beautiful 300-year-old Basque farmhouse, a couple of kilometres north of Gernika, or outdoors in the garden, it's a great spot to enjoy traditional dishes roasted in a wood-fired oven.

Boliña El Viejo € *Adolfo Urioste 1, tel: 94 625 10 15,* www.restaurante bolinaelviejo.com. Old-fashioned, very local bar-restaurant that's the best-value place to eat in the centre of Gernika. Traditional favourites in its simple *comedor* include grilled fish, beans and squid in ink.

SAN SEBASTIÁN

Arzak €€€ *Avda. Alcalde Elósegui 273, tel: 94 327 84 65,* www.arzak.es. What might look like a typical family-owned *taberna*, on the lower slopes of Monte Ulia 3km east of the centre, is in fact the crucible of Basque *nueva cocina*, triple-starred by Michelin. Father-and-daughter team Juan Mari and Elena Arzak prepare a different selection of stunningly creative dishes each day, with the set menu costing more than a hotel room – look out especially for pigeon or lamb. Behind the scenes, a fully fledged research lab is hard at work developing new concoctions. Closed Mon.

Borda Berri €€ *Fermín Calbetón, 12 tel: 94 343 03 42.* Rustic, inviting old-town pintxos place, with yellow walls, almost no seating, and eager crowds of in-the-know tourists. There's no food on display; everything on the changing blackboard menu is cooked to order, in substantial starter-size portions. Closed Mon and Tue.

Goiz Argi € *Fermín Calbetón 4, tel: 94 342 52 04.* Popular Casco Viejo pintxos bar with a contemporary edge. It's deservedly renowned for its prawn brochettes. Closed Tue.

Itxaropena €–€€ *Embeltrán 16, tel: 94 342 45 76,* www.baritxaropena. com. Charming, cosy old-town cider-house restaurant that serves hearty, high-quality traditional cuisine on menus ranging from a cheaper one offering paella, squid in ink, and dessert, plus cider to a more expensive one, which includes lobster with rice. Closed Mon.

Martín Berasategui €€€ *Loidi 4, Lasarte-Oria, tel: 94 336 64 71,* www. martinberasategui.com. Contemporary rather than molecular, this three-star Michelin restaurant is housed in a bright modern structure in the hills 10km southwest of the city. Its eponymous chef remains rooted in traditional Spanish cuisine, with the addition of his own subtle twists. Closed Mon and Tue.

Txepetxa € *Pescadería 5, tel: 94 342 22 27,* www.bartxepetxa.com. While this old-town bar offers a full range of pintxos, almost everyone's here for just one thing – its out-of-this-world anchovies, served on toast with everything from foie gras to grated coconut. Closed Mon.

VITORIA

Asador €–€€ *Sagartoki Prado 18, tel: 94 528 86 76,* www.sagartoki.com. The best pintxos in the city – beautiful to look at, and delicious to eat. Be sure to try the egg-yolk parcels, or the foie gras cornets. On weekdays, you can sample five, plus a glass of wine, for a set price; they also offer full dinner menus.

Ikea €€–€€€ *Portal de Castilla 27, tel: 94 514 47 47,* www.restauranteikea.com. This is Vitoria's most acclaimed restaurant, a chic and expensive dining room in a stone townhouse transformed by designer Javier Mariscal. It serves good Basque food with a contemporary spin. The liver pâté is recommended. Closed Mon.

La Malquerida € *Correría 10, tel: 94 525 70 68,* www.lamalqueridavitoria.com. Popular tapas bar a few steps away from the Plaza de la Virgen Blanca. The chalked-up menu of innovative snacks and *raciónes* can be enjoyed both indoors and out, with crowds spilling into the adjoining alleyways.

El Portalón €€€ *Correría 150, tel: 94 514 27 55,* www.restauranteelportalon.com. Vitoria's most beautiful sixteenth-century house makes an atmospheric setting. They specialise in traditional Basque cooking and also serve pintxos at weekends.

Saburdi € *Dato 32, tel: 94 514 70 16,* www.saburdi.com. Busy, friendly tapas bar, with outdoor tables on the main pedestrian road up from the station. Great-value pintxos – try the cod with squash, or quail's egg with ham – plus more substantial *raciónes*.

A-Z TRAVEL TIPS

A SUMMARY OF PRACTICAL INFORMATION

A

ACCOMMODATION

The official tourist website, www.bilbaoturismo.net, has a range of information about accommodation, including hotels, hostels, guesthouses and apartments; there is also a useful central booking service (tel: 946 941 212). If you are looking for a budget hotel, the nicest place to stay has to be the **Casco Viejo,** although it is liable to be noisy at night. Bilbao's luxury hotels tend to be scattered across **Ensanche**; many feature hip contemporary architecture and highly regarded restaurants, and can be amazingly good value. **Deusto** and **Castaños**, on the river's north bank, make good alternatives. You'll need to book well ahead for the summer months, especially if there is a fiesta or other big event on.

AIRPORTS

Bilbao's airport, the **Aeropuerto de Bilbao** (www.aena.es/es/aeropuerto-bilbao/index.html) is 12km north of town. Bizkaiabus A-3247 (www.bizkaia.eus) runs every 30mins (roughly) to Termibús station (Metro: San Mamés), stopping on the Gran Via. The journey to the centre takes about 20 minutes. The alternative is a taxi (tel: 944 800 909; www.taxisaeropuertobilbao.com) which will cost around €30, but depending on traffic, this might not be that much quicker than the bus. There are also hourly buses straight to San Sebastián, which also has a small airport (www.aena.es/es/aeropuerto-san-sebastian/index.html).

B

BICYCLE RENTAL

Several companies hire bikes and other wheeled vehicles for the day. Central Bilbao is flat and easy to get around by bike (see page 90).

BUDGETING FOR YOUR TRIP

As a rough guide, if you stay in a youth hostel or cheap hotel; walk as much as you can and use public transport sparingly; and stick to local restaurants, then you could get by on between €50 and €80 a day. Alternatively, if you want to stay somewhere a bit more stylish or comfortable; eat in fancier restaurants; and go out on the town; then you'll need more like €100–150 a day. Of course, if you opt for a five-star hotel, this figure won't even cover your room.

If you are going to be using public transport a lot it may be worth buying a 24-hour, 48-hour or 72-hour tourist card (www.bilbaobizkaia card.com) which gives you unlimited use of metros, trams, buses and funicular as well as discounted entry to sights.

After accommodation, food is likely to be the biggest item in your budget. During weekday lunchtimes all restaurants offer a *menu del día* that is much less expensive (perhaps as little as €10 for three courses) than eating a la carte. Look for restaurants away from tourist areas where the locals eat. The price of the menu del día is normally posted outside on the street. Pintxos (tapas) can be an economical way to eat a light meal, especially in the evening, but choose an ordinary neighbourhood bar – not one with gourmet pretensions.

A typical museum entry fee will be about €10. If you are on a tight budget, you can still build your sightseeing around mostly free sights.

C

CAR HIRE

You won't need a car for visiting Bilbao but if you want to explore the hinterland and not be dependent on public transport – or go where public transport doesn't reach – you will need a hire car. You must be over 21 to do this. You'll have to decide how much damage waiver you are willing to pay: the more risk you take on yourself, the cheaper the day rate will be. It is cheaper to book a pre-paid package before you travel. When you collect your car you will need a driving licence valid in Spain and a credit card against which a deposit will be held until you return the car without damage.

CLIMATE

Being on the Atlantic coast and part of the so-called "Green Spain", Bilbao gets a lot of rain. The city has a humid oceanic climate with prevailing westerly winds creating moderate rather than extreme temperatures averaging 8° in winter and 20° in summer.

CLOTHING

Even in summer, it is wise to pack a sweater for cool evenings and a light coat – especially if you intend to go on excursions out of the city. It is prudent to have a waterproof or umbrella with you.

CRIME AND SAFETY

There are no dangerous places in central Bilbao but it is best not want to wander around unfamiliar streets in the suburbs late at night.

Pickpocketing and bag-snatching is, unfortunately, a fact of life in a touristy city like Bilbao, though no more so than anywhere else in Europe. You need to be on guard in crowded places and on public transport, but there's no need to be paranoid. Taking the usual sensible precautions should help keep your stay safe. Know where your belongings are at all times (don't leave bags unattended, even if you're looking at rooms upstairs in a hostal). Keep an eye on your handbag; don't put wallets in your back pocket; leave passport and tickets in the hotel safe; and keep a photocopy of your passport, plus notes of your credit card helplines and so on. Don't leave anything in view in a parked car.

On the street, beware of people standing unusually close at street kiosks or attractions, or of those trying to distract you for any reason (pointing out "bird poo" – in reality, planted shaving cream – on your jacket, shoving a card or paper to read right under your nose). Next thing you know, your wallet has gone.

If you do get robbed, go straight to the police, where you'll need to make an official statement (known as a *denuncia*), not least because your insurance company will require a police report. Expect it to be a time-consuming and laborious business – you can do it online (details on www.policia.es), but you'll still have to go into the station to sign it. If you have your passport stolen, you will need to contact your embassy or consulate.

D

DRIVING

Everywhere worth seeing in Bilbao can be reached either on foot or using public transport. The main sights outside the city are accessible by bus or train. You won't need to hire a car unless you want to explore the countryside, or be entirely free of timetables.

Road signs are European standard designs.

The police are strict about regulations to do with speeding, drink driving and mobile phone use. Being a foreigner is no excuse.

The Basque Country has a good road network. A few remote back roads may be in bad repair but all main roads are well-maintained and reliable. N (carretera nacional) roads, marked red on the map, are to be used by preference for fast travel. "Yellow" roads are generally slower and more scenic. The best roads are *autopistas*, four lane highways for which you pay a toll, and *autovias*, similarly with two lanes in each direction but toll-free. Don't be too ambitious about how many miles you cover on a touring holiday: in this corner of Spain many roads have endless sharp bends and they frequently cross mountain passes.

E

ELECTRICITY

Plugs in Spain are of the two-prong, standard European type. The current in Spain is 220v – bring an adaptor (and transformer) to use UK and US laptops, mobile phone chargers, and other electronic devices.

EMBASSIES AND CONSULATES

The embassies of the UK, USA, Canada, Australia, New Zealand, Ireland

and South Africa are in Madrid.

EMERGENCIES
112 All emergency services
092 Municipal police
061 Ambulance
080 Fire service
062 Law Enforcement (Guardia Civil)
091 Police (Policía Nacional)

G

GETTING THERE
By Plane
Bilbao airport is served by around 20 airlines, including Iberia, British Airways, Easyjet, Ryanair and Aer Lingus. There are flights from London and other UK airports, Dublin and many European cities. To get to Bilbao from the US or Australia you will need to fly into either Madrid or Barcelona and take a connecting domestic flight, or a train.

By ferry
Brittany Ferries (www.brittany-ferries.co.uk) sail from Portsmouth (in the UK) one to three times weekly, carrying vehicles and passengers into Bilbao's ferry port, Zierbena. The port is 21km northwest of the city centre, but there are regular buses and trains which run from the docks to the centre.

By train
To get to Bilbao from the UK by train, take the Eurostar from London St Pancras to Paris Gare du Nord. Transfer to Montparnasse station by Metro and catch the high speed train south to Hendaye. There you need to switch to the Euskotren which takes you to San Sebastián, where you will need to spend the night. From San Sebastián's Amara station the narrow gauge line continues to Bilbao, with trains stopping at two stations, Zazpi Kaleak or Matiko. For details of this journey see www.

oui.sncf and. www.euskotren.eus. An excellent site for European rail information is www.seat61.com.

By Coach

A Eurolines (www.eurolines.eu) coach will get you to Bilbao 24 hours after leaving London, with a change in Paris.

By Car

The fastest route from London to Bilbao takes approximately 14 hours to cover the 1400km and uses mainly toll motorways to get through France. It passes via the Channel Tunnel, Rouen, Tours, Poitiers, Bordeaux, Hendaye and San Sebastián.

GUIDES AND TOURS

Guided tours are available, including to several particular buildings including the Iberdrola Tower, the Palacio Euskalduna, Azkuna Zentro, the Teatro Arriaga and the city hall. For details see the tourist information office's website: www.bilbaoturismo.net or www.triptobasque-country.com.

H

HEALTH AND MEDICAL CARE

The **European Health Insurance Card (EHIC)** gives EU citizens access to Spanish state public-health services under reciprocal agreements. While this will provide free or reduced-cost medical care in the event of minor injuries and emergencies, it won't cover every eventuality – and it only applies to EU citizens in possession of the card – so travel insurance is essential. If the UK leaves the EU, Britons will have to make other arrangements; check www.gov.uk for updates.

No **inoculations** are required for Spain, and the worst that's likely to happen to you is that you might fall victim to an upset stomach. To be safe, wash fruit and avoid tapas dishes that look as if they were prepared last week. Water at public fountains is fine, unless there's a sign saying "agua no potable", in which case don't drink it.

For minor complaints, go to a **farmacia** – pharmacists are highly trained, willing to give advice (often in English) and able to dispense many drugs that would be available only on prescription in other countries. They keep usual shop hours (Mon–Fri 9am–1.30pm & 5–8pm), but some open late and at weekends, while a rota system (displayed in the window of every pharmacy) keeps at least one open 24 hours in every town.

If you have special medical or dietary requirements, it is advisable to carry a letter from your doctor, translated into Spanish, indicating the nature of your condition and necessary treatments. With luck, you'll get the address of an English-speaking **doctor** from the nearest farmacia, police station or tourist office – it's obviously more likely in resorts and big cities. Treatment at **hospitals** for EU citizens in possession of the EHIC card is free; otherwise, you'll be charged at private-hospital rates, which can be very expensive.

L

LANGUAGE

The Basque Country has two official languages: Spanish (commonly called Castilian) and Basque (Euskera). Both are used in everyday life, but many people who work with tourists speak English.

You will hear Basque widely spoken but almost everyone will be willing to switch to Spanish if necessary. Street names and signs are invariably bilingual. Only very occasionally in the countryside outside the city will you find Basque spoken exclusively.

Spanish is a phonetic language: words are pronounced exactly as they are spelt. It uses two verbs to mean "to be" and has two ways for one person to address another, formal and informal.

LGBTQ TRAVELLERS

Bilbao prides itself on being extremely LGBTQ-friendly. It is entirely normal for same-sex couples to hold hands, kiss or show signs of affection in public places – except in churches, where it is prudent to be discreet.

There are various bars, restaurants and clubs where the LGBTQ community frequent, especially in the Casco Viejo. Spain was the third country in the world to legalise same-sex marriage – in 2005. The tourist information office provides LGBTQ information at www.bilbaoturismo.net/Bilbao Turismo/es/lgbt_2. The online magazine Pride Everywhere (http://issuu.com/turismobilbao/docs/lgbt_eng) is an introduction to gay life in Bilbao. Another useful website is www.bilbaobizkaiapride.com

M

MEDIA

The most read Spanish national daily newspapers are the centre-left El País (elpais.es) and the centre-right El Mundo (elmundo.es), both of which have good arts and foreign news coverage, including comprehensive regional "what's on" listings and supplements every weekend. Another big seller is the right of centre ABC. The main regional papers in the Basque Country are El Correo, Deia and Gara. The paper with the highest circulation, however, is Marca, the country's top sports daily.

There are many radio stations to tune into. The state-run Radio Nacional de España, or RNE (rtve.es/radio) has five stations: Radio Nacional, a general news and information channel; Radio Clásica, broadcasting mainly classical music and related programmes; the popular music channel Radio 3; Radio 4, in Catalan; and the rolling news and sports channel Radio 5. Other popular channels include Cadena Ser and Onda Cero (news, talk, sports and culture); the Catholic Church-run COPE; Los 40 Principales (for the latest hits); Cadena 100 (music and cultural programming) and Radio Marca (dedicated to sports).

RTV (http://rtve.es/television) provides the main, state-run television channels, namely La 1 (ie, "Uno"), a general entertainment and news channel, and its sister La 2 ("Dos"). Private national stations are Antena 3, Cuatro (Four), Telecinco (Five) and La Sexta (Sixth). The Basque Country also has its own ETB channels (in Basque). The main satellite channel is Canal+.

MONEY

Spain's currency is the **euro** (€), with notes issued in denominations of 5, 10, 20, 50, 100, 200 and 500 euros, and coins in denominations of 1, 2, 5, 10, 20 and 50 cents, and 1 and 2 euros.

By far the easiest way to get money is to use your bank debit card to withdraw cash from an ATM, found all over the city, as well as on arrival at the airport. You can usually withdraw up to €300 a day, and instructions are offered in English once you insert your card. Make sure you have a personal identification number (PIN) that's designed to work overseas, and take a note of your bank's emergency contact number in case the machine swallows your card. Some European debit cards can also be used directly in shops to pay for purchases; you'll need to check first with your bank.

All major credit cards are accepted in hotels, restaurants and shops, and for tours, tickets and transport, though don't count on being able to use them in every small bar. If you use a foreign credit card in some shops, you may also be asked for photo ID, so be prepared to show a driving licence or passport. Make sure you make a note of the number for reporting lost or stolen cards to your credit card company.

Spanish banks are usually open Monday to Friday 8.30am to 2pm, with some city branches open Saturday 8.30am to 1pm (except June–Sept when all banks close on Sat), although times can vary from bank to bank. Outside these times, it's usually possible to change cash at larger hotels (generally with bad rates and high commission) or with travel agents – useful for small amounts in a hurry.

O

OPENING TIMES

Traditionally shops, museums, churches, tourist offices and other offices in Spain have always closed for at least two hours in the middle part of the day but increasingly in cosmopolitan cities such as Bilbo they conform to continuous opening hours. Generally it is safe to assume an opening time of 10am and because life goes on later in the day than in other European countries, many places will close at 8pm, 10pm or even later. most places are open on Saturday and many on Sunday too. Most museums close for one day in the week.

P

POLICE

The police in Spain come in various guises. The **Guardia Civil**, in green uniforms, are a national police force, formerly a military organization, that have responsibility for national crime, as well as roads, borders and guarding public buildings. Locally, most policing is carried out by the **Policía Municipal**, who wear blue-and-white uniforms, and these tend to be the most approachable if you're reporting a crime, for example. The Basque Country also has its own police force, the **Ertzaintza** (blue and red, with red berets) who you're most likely to encounter on traffic duty. The Ertzaintza has police stations at Calle Ibarrekolanda 9 and Calle Autonomía, 1. The Municipal Police are based on Plaza Ernesto Erkoreka and Calle Carlos de Gortázar, 3.

POST OFFICES

Post offices (Correos; correos.es) are normally open weekdays from 8am to 2pm and again from 5pm to 7.30pm, though branches in bigger places may have longer hours, may not close at midday and may open on Saturday mornings. There's an office-finder on the website, which also gives exact opening hours and contact details for each post office in Spain. As you can also pay bills and buy phonecards in post offices, queues can be long – it's often easier to buy **stamps** at tobacconists (look for the brown-and-yellow estanco sign).

Post boxes are bright yellow. Outbound mail is reasonably reliable, with letters or cards taking around three days to a week to the UK and the rest of Europe, a week to ten days to North America, New Zealand and Australia, although it can be more erratic in the summer.

PUBLIC HOLIDAYS

The following public holidays are observed in the Basque Country. On these days shops and sights are likely to be closed:

Jan 1 Año Nuevo, New Year's Day

Jan 6 Epifanía, Epiphany

March 19 Feast Day of Saint Joseph

Holy Thursday

March/April Viernes Santo, Good Friday, Easter Monday

May 1 Fiesta del Trabajo, May Day

Jul 25 Feast Day of St James

Aug 15 La Asunción, Assumption of the Virgin

Oct 12 Día de la Hispanidad, National Day

Nov 1 Todos los Santos, All Saints

Dec 6 Día de la Constitución, Constitution Day

Dec 8 Inmaculada Concepción

Dec 25 Navidad, Christmas Day

August is traditionally Spain's holiday month, when many of the locals go away and tourists move in. Some shops close for the month. In contrast, it can prove nearly impossible to find a room especially during Bilbao's main annual fiesta, the Aste Nagusia/Semana Grande. Similarly, seats on planes, trains and buses in August should if possible be booked in advance.

R

RELIGION

Spain is a predominantly Catholic country and although church attendance has fallen steadily over the last few decades there are still many believers in the Basque Country. Loyalty to local saints continues into the present day and most traditional festivals incorporate a religious element. Other denominations and religions also have places of worship in Bilbao.

T

TELEPHONES

Spanish **telephone numbers** have nine digits; mobile numbers begin with a 6 or 7, freephone numbers begin 900, while other 90-plus- and 80-plus-digit numbers are nationwide standard-rate or special-rate services. To **call Spain from abroad**, dial your country's international access code + 34 (Spain's country code) + the nine-digit Spanish number.

Public telephones have instructions in English, and accept coins, credit cards and phonecards.

Most European **mobile phones** will work in Spain, though it's worth checking with your provider whether you need to get international access switched on. By European law, EU mobile phone companies are not allowed to charge extra roaming fees for using a mobile (including text and data services) in another EU nation.

Calling home from Spain, you dial 00 (Spain's international access code) + your country code (44 for the UK) + city/area code minus initial zero + number. For **reverse-charge calls**, dial the international operator (tel: 1008 for Europe or 1005 for the rest of the world).

TIME ZONES

Spain is one hour ahead of the UK's GMT; six hours ahead of Eastern Standard Time; nine hours ahead of Pacific Standard Time; eight hours behind Australia; ten hours behind New Zealand; and the same time as South Africa. The clocks go forward in the last week in March and move back again in the last week in October, but this adjustment is likely to come to an end in 2021 when a EU directive comes into force.

TIPPING

There are no rules on tipping in Spain. In informal circumstances, such as after eating in cheap restaurants, it is common to round the bill up to the nearest whole euro. In more expensive restaurants you may want to reward good service with a couple of euros or even a generous 10 percent of the bill. Taxi drivers don't expect anything unless you particularly want to say thank you. In well-to-do hotels it will be appropriate to tip someone who carries your bag or to leave two or three euros for the room service.

TOILETS

Public toilets are generally reasonably clean but don't always have any paper. are most commonly referred to and labelled Los Servicios, though signs may point you to baños, aseos or lavabos. Damas (Ladies) and Caballeros (Gentlemen) are the usual distinguishing signs for sex, though you may also see the potentially confusing Señoras (Women) and Señores (Men).

TOURIST INFORMATION

Turismo Bilbao (www.bilbaoturismo.net) has tourist offices at Plaza Circular 1 at the end of the Gran Via (tel: 94 479 57 60; daily 9am–8pm), and on Alameda Mazzaredo (next to the Museo Guggenheim; Mon–Sat 10am–7pm, Sun 10–3pm). For information about San Sebastián, see www.sansebastianturismoa.eus/en; for the rest of the Basque Country, see www.tourism.euskadi.eus/en, and for travelling in Spain in general, see www.spain.info.

TRANSPORT

Walking

Central Bilbao is small enough to walk around comfortably; indeed, the riverside stroll between the Casco Viejo and the Guggenheim is a high-light for many visitors.

Metro

The easy, efficient Metro Bilbao (www.metrobilbao.eus; tel: 94 425 40 25) consists of three lines. Line 1 runs between Extebarri, south of the centre, and Plentzia (northeast of Getxo) – handy for the beach. Across the ria, Line 3 goes out to Santurtzi at the western rivermouth. Line 3, accessed from the Casco Viejo, is shorter and much less useful for tourists. The Metro runs from 6am to 11pm with a train every 6 minutes at peak times.

If you're staying for any length of time, consider buying a pay-as-you-go *Barik* card, which can be topped up to any amount.

The Metro is considered a tourist attraction in its own right. Its stations were designed by Norman Foster and the street-level glass entrances are known as *fosteritos*.

Urban buses

For parts the Metro doesn't reach, there are red municipal buses operated by **Bilbobus** (www.bilbao.eus/cs/Satellite/bilbobus/es/inicio; tel: 94 479 09 81) which operates from 6am to 11pm. Maps of the 35 daytime and eight night-time routes are posted at the green bus shelters.

Tram

A single tram line links the Casco Viejo and the Museo Guggenheim with San Mamés and the bus station. It is operated by Eusoktren (www.euskotren.eus; tel: 94 433 33 30).

Long distance buses

Long-distance and international bus companies use the Termibús station (termibus.es; tel: 94 439 50 77), which fills an entire block between Luis Briñas and Gurtubay. To reach the town centre from the bus station, change onto a local bus, head a block north to the San Mamés Metro station or simply walk.

Destinations served include: Bermeo, via Gernika and Mundaka (30 daily; 1hr 10min); Castro Urdiales (5 daily; 1hr); Elantxobe (3 daily; 1hr 30min); Lekeitio (5 daily; 1hr 30min); Oñati (3 daily; 1hr 10min); Ondarroa (20 daily; 1hr 20min); San Sebastián (every 30min; 1hr 15min); and Vitoria (every 30min; 1hr 15min).

Train

There are three different rail companies (using separate stations) which operate out of Bilbao:

Estación de Abando. The main RENFE train station (www.renfe.com), on Pza. Circular, across the river from the Casco Viejo, sees services to Barcelona (2 daily; 6hr 50min); Logroño (2 daily; 2hr 30min); Madrid (4 daily; 5–7hr); and Salamanca (3 daily; 6hr). There are also commuter trains.

Estación de la Concordia. Services along a separate narrow-gauge line, run by RENFE and formerly known as FEVE (www.renfe.com/viajeros/feve), head west along the coast from this highly decorative station, also known as the Estación de Santander, on the riverbank below the Estación de Abando, to Santander (3 daily; 3hr) and beyond.

Estación de Atxuri. South of the Casco Viejo on the right bank of the river, the Estación de Atxuri is used by frequent EuskoTren (www.euskotren.eus) trains to San Sebastián (2hr 40min), Guernica (45min), Mundaka (1hr 10min), and Bermeo (1hr 15min).

By taxi

TeleTaxi tel: 94 410 21 21, www.teletaxibilbao.com; Radio Taxi Bilbao tel: 94 444 88 88, www.taxibilbao.com.

Funiculars

There are two funiculars in or near Bilbao. One is up to Artxanda. The other, inland from Portugalete and Santurzi, climbs to Lareineta (operated by Euskotren).

Bilbao Bizkaia Card

The Bilbao Bizkaia card (www.bilbaobizcaiacard.com) is valid for 24, 48 or 72 hours. Once activated, it gives unlimited use of all forms of public transport: Metro, tram Euskotren trains, coaches (Bizkaibus), and even the two funiculars of Bilbao (Artxanda and Lareineta). It also gives you faster access to the Guggenheim (but you still have to pay the entrance fee) and allows you to join official tourist office guided tours for free. However, if you are going to be mostly walking and only intend taking the odd Metro or bus ride, you will be much better off with a Barik card, topping it up as needed.

TRAVELLERS WITH DISABILITIES

Spain, as a modern European country, aims to make all public places (sights, hotels, restaurants, offices) accessible to wheelchair users and anyone with any form of disability. By law, such places must be equipped with ramps and lifts; more importantly, there is increasing awareness of the need to offer help for any kind of difference. Things are not perfect in

Bilbao but staff will usually be willing to give assistance if you state your requirements. The tourist office gives some information on www.bilbao-turismo.net/BilbaoTurismo/en/accessible-tourism. The more advance planning you do, the better your trip will be. Useful websites for this include Travel for All (www.travelforall.es/accesible-travel/?lang=en) and **Tourism For All** (www.tourism forall.org.uk).

V

VISAS AND ENTRY REQUIREMENTS

EU citizens (and those of Norway, Iceland, Liechtenstein and Switzerland) need only a valid national identity card or passport to enter Spain. Other Europeans, and citizens of the **United States**, **Canada**, **Australia** and **New Zealand**, require a passport but no visa, and can stay as a tourist for up to ninety days. Other nationalities (including South Africans) will need to get a visa from a Spanish embassy or consulate before departure. As visa requirements can change, it's always advisable to check the current situation before leaving home.

W

WEBSITES AND INTERNET ACCESS

By far the best website for information on Bilbao is that which is run by the official tourist office, www.bilbaoturismo.net. Also useful (such as for downloadable maps) is the council's site, www.bilbao.eus (eus being the suffix for Euskadi- the Basque Country). www.Sietecallesbilbao.net has some useful information about the Casco Viejo, while www.bizkaia. net has information on Bilbao's beaches.

The website www.visitbiscay.eus is good for information about places around Bilbao, while www.Tourism.euskadi.eus is the site for the Basque Country in general. You can check out www.sansebastianturis-moa.eus, which is the official site for San Sebastián, and www.vitoria-gasteiz.org for Vitoria.

RECOMMENDED HOTELS

Bilbao's upmarket hotels are mostly in the Ensanche and Abandoibarra areas; some are monuments of contemporary architecture in their own right. If you want somewhere with more character, you will want to be in the Casco Viejo where there are more budget choices. Given the small size of the city, any of these three areas will make a suitable base for sightseeing.

Another option is to stay on the coast and commute into the city for sightseeing. Book ahead for peak periods when Spain is on holiday – especially Easter Week and in August. The tourist information office website (www.bilbaoturismo.net) has details of hotels, hostels, guesthouses (traditionally called *pensiones*) and apartments. The official accommodation reservation service can be contacted on tel: 946 941 212.

€€€€€	over 250 euros
€€€€	150–200 euros
€€€	100–150 euros
€€	50–100 euros
€	under 50 euros

CASCO VIEJO

7Kale €€ *Santa Maria 13 Andra Maria kale, tel: 94 640 20 11*, www.7kalebnb.com. A friendly bed and breakfast with 12 rooms, including 2 triples. You get a free mug if you book directly from the website.

Caravan Cinema €€€ *Correo 11, tel: 68 886 09 07,* www.caravan-cinema.com. Each room in this comfortable little boutique hotel, just off the main square, celebrates a specific movie director, with all relevant films pre-loaded to the TV. Five, including "Pedro Almodóvar", are normal-sized doubles, but the real joy is the retro-furnished, two-room Hitchcock apartment, which sleeps up to seven guests.

Casual Bilbao Gurea €€ *Bidebarrieta 14, tel: 94 416 32 99,* www.casual hoteles.com. The simple, clean rooms in this well-kept hotel are a great deal – and surprisingly peaceful – for such a central location, while the staff are exceptionally helpful.

Estrella Ostatu €€ *María Muñoz 6, Tel 94 416 40 66,* www.la-estrella-ostatu.com. If you just want a simple place to lay your head and in a good location for walking to the sights, this *pensión* near Plaza Unamuno will give you no-nonsense service at a decent price.

Iturrienea Ostatua €€ *Santa María 14, tel: 94 416 15 00,* www.iturrienea ostatua.com. Clean, very friendly hotel, tucked away near the river in the Casco Viejo, with exposed stonework and antique furniture throughout; the walls are hung with quirky art and moody photos of Bilbao's industrial past. All nine rooms are en suite; many have plants trailing over balconies, and double-glazing to cut down noise.

Quartier Bilbao Hostel €–€€ *Artekale 15, tel: 94 497 88 00,* www.quartier bilbao.com. Modern and very central hostel, just up from the river, offering private doubles as well as dorms holding from two to ten beds; one storey is reserved for women only. There's also a communal kitchen and terrace.

Tayko €€€ *Calle de la Ribera 13, (erribera kalea), tel: 94 465 20 70,* www. taykohotels.com. A boutique "lifestyle" hotel in which you can choose between a room with a river view or one with a street view. There is a restaurant and a gastrobar. As with all Casco Viejo hotels, the problem is parking; the hotel can help you to find a space, but it won't be nearby.

ENSANCHE

Art Lodge Bilbao €€€ *Iturriza 3, tel: 94 685 89 51,* www.bilbaoartlodge. com. As the name suggests, art is the theme of this *pensión* besides Abando station. There are only six rooms, each named after an art form: architecture, sculpture, dance, literature, music, and painting. Works by young Basque artists are displayed on the walls.

Begoña €€ *Amistad 2, 1º, tel: 94 423 01 34,* www.hostalbegona.com. Solid mid-range option, near the narrow-gauge station and just a couple of minutes' walk over the bridge from the Casco Viejo. The colourful rooms have lino floors, good en-suite facilities, and comfortable beds, but no views.

Carlton €€€ *Plaza Moyúa 2, tel: 94 416 22 00,* www.hotelcarlton.es. The *grande dame* of Bilbao hotels, built in 1919 and still an atmospheric place to stay, with its abundant marble and dramatic stained-glass cupola. The rooms are tasteful and extremely comfortable, and several boast huge arched windows.

Zubia Urban Rooms € *Amistad 5, tel: 944 248 566,* www.pensionzubia. com. Veteran family-run hotel, near the left bank of the river across from the Casco Viejo, where the plain modernized rooms share bathrooms. The friendly staff are more than happy to share their local expertise; pets are welcome.

ABANDOIBARRA

Cosmov €€ *Rekalde Zumarkalea 12–14, tel: 94 401 54 54,* www.cosmovhotel bilba.com. Perhaps the cheapest option if you want to stay in Abandoibarra, the Cosmov is on the road between the Plaza Moyua and the Guggenheim Museum. It has 28 rooms divided into basic, standard, family and superior.

Gran Hotel Domine €€€ *Alameda de Mazarredo 61, tel: 94 425 33 00,* www. hoteldominebilbao.com. The work of designer Javier Mariscal, this is a wonderfully inspiring five-star hotel, appropriately close to the Guggenheim and sporting one of the most imaginative lobbies you'll ever see. Each floor has a unique design, while the luxurious rooms have bathrooms with transparent glass, and tubs designed by Philippe Starck.

Meliá Bilbao €€€ *Lehendakari Leizaola 29, tel: 944 280 000,* www.melia. com. One of Bilbao's most distinctive buildings, a bold edifice inspired by Eduardo Chillida, utilizing Iranian pink marble and rusty garnet tones for the exterior, and green and white marble in the bathrooms. The stylish rooms are luxurious, with huge, incredibly comfy beds; there's also a pool.

Miró €€€€ *Alameda de Mazarredo 77, tel: 94 661 18 80*, www.mirohotel bilbao.com. Attractive fifty-room hotel, with minimalist decor, bathrooms finished in black marble (and separated from the chic, white-toned rooms by a curtain) and a decent spa.

Vincci Consulado de Bilbao €€€ *Alameda Mazarredo, tel: 94 644 20 61*, www.vincciconsuladodebilbao.com. The closest place to stay near the Guggenheim, with a terrace from which you can gaze on Frank Gehry's architecture while you sip a cocktail. Restaurant and private parking is available.

NORTH OF THE RIVER

Bilbao Akelarre Hostel €–€€ *Morgan 4–6, tel: 94 405 77 13*, www.bilbao akelarrehostel.com. Modern, well-run and well-equipped hostel near the university, a short walk from the Guggenheim. There are a few double rooms – albeit with individual bunks – plus dorms sleeping from four to twelve. Rates include breakfast, coffee and tea.

NH Collection €€€ *Ría de Bilbao Paseo Campo de Volantín 28, tel: 94 405 11 00*, www.nh-hotels.com. Smart, modern riverfront hotel, in a funky contemporary building fronted by pastel-coloured glassed-in balconies. The sizeable rooms have sleek minimalist furnishings, and there's on-site parking. Close to the Zubizuri footbridge.

BASQUE COAST

Caserio Arboliz €€ *Arboliz 12, Elantxobe, tel: 94 627 62 83*, www.arboliz. com. This conspicuous white-painted house, perched on the clifftop in Ibarrangelu, 1km southeast of Elantxobe, has been converted into a comfortable rural *agroturismo*, with kitchen facilities available, and a lovely sea-view garden.

El Puerto €€–€€€ *Portu 1, Mundaka, tel: 94 687 67 25*, www.hotelelpuerto.com. This delightful hotel faces out to sea from right beside the fishing port, and has a lovely shaded terrace. Several of its en-suite rooms have great sea views. Be warned that it's liable to be noisy at night in summer.

Saiaz Getaria €€€ *Roke 25–27, Getaria, tel: 94 314 01 43,* www.saiazgetaria. com. Magnificent fifteenth-century mansion, topped by formidable stone towers, and stylishly converted to hold seventeen exceptionally comfortable bedrooms. It is worth paying more for a room with a sea view.

Torre €€ *Ercilla Talaranzko 14, 1º, Bermeo tel: 94 618 75 98,* www.hoteltxaraka.com. Inexpensive accommodation a few streets up from the port behind Santa María church. Ask for the spacious corner room, which has a balcony and glassed-in gallery as well as an en-suite bathroom.

Zubieta €€€ *Portal de Atea, Lekeitio, tel: 94 684 30 30,* www.hotelzubieta. com. Charming, very elegant hotel, set in the gardens of an old palace at the inland end of town, out in the fields but just 650m from the harbour. Bright, well-furnished en-suite rooms and excellent breakfasts.

GERNIKA

Gernika €€ *Carlos Gangoiti 17, tel: 94 625 03 50,* www.hotel-gernika. com. Gernika's largest and most comfortable hotel is north of the centre, 500m along the road towards Bermeo. There's nothing remarkable about its forty en-suite rooms, but they're reasonably well kept and quiet.

Pensión Akelarre Ostatua €€ *Barrenkale 5, tel: 94 627 01 97,* www.hotel akelarre.com. Cheap central *pensión*, right behind the *turismo*, with seventeen plain but brightly painted rooms equipped with showers. The front desk is closed 1–6pm, and after 9pm, but you can check in by inserting a credit card next to the door.

SAN SEBASTIAN

Amaiur €€ *31 de Agosto 44, 2º, tel: 94 342 96 54,* www.pensionamaiur. com. Classic old-style budget hotel, in a venerable house deep in the warren-like streets of the old town. Rooms differ in size – some sleep four – and are decorated in widely varying styles. Some have en-suite bathrooms and private balconies, others share bathrooms, and there are two communal kitchens.

Casa Nicolasa €€€€ *Aldamar 4, 1º; tel: 94 343 01 43*, www.pensioncasa nicolasa.com. Impeccable and unusually large modern rooms, with spacious bathrooms, in a relatively peaceful location facing the market place in the old town.

Londres y de Inglaterra €€€€€ *Zubieta 2, tel: 94 344 07 70*, www.h londres.com. The very welcoming *grande dame* of San Sebastián hotels, this impressive white nineteenth-century edifice commands a superb position overlooking the beach, a short walk from the old town. Live it up in style in a spacious, very comfortable room with huge seafront windows. Look for good low-season offers.

María Cristina €€€€€ *Paseo Republica Argentina 4, tel: 94 343 76 00*, www.hotel-mariacristina.com. Landmark hotel, dominating the rivermouth near the edge of the old town, that's the epicentre of September's film festival. Refurbished to mark its centenary in 2012, its sumptuous *belle époque* rooms are the last word in old-style luxury, boasting huge beds and opulent bathrooms.

Pensión Edorta €€ *Puerto 15, 1º, tel: 94 342 37 73*, www.pensionedorta. com. Welcoming family-run hotel, upstairs in a historic house in the heart of the old town, just up from the harbour. Bright, attractive rooms abound in period charm, with exposed stonework and ancient beams. The cheapest share bathrooms and lack even washbasins; book ahead, and pay up to €35 extra, for your own top-quality bathroom.

La Perla €€ *Loiola 10, 1º, tel: 94 390 04 75*, www.pensionlaperla.com. Great-value new-town *pensión*, handy for bus and train stations as well as the old town and beach. Friendly service and simple but spacious rooms, all en suite and some with balconies. Dogs are allowed here and

Regil €€ *Easo 9, 1º, tel: 94 342 71 43*, www.pensionregil.com. Eight neat, tidy but rather small rooms, in a great location near the beach and old town, with extremely helpful management. They offer three room types: queen-size, twins and singles.

RIOJA

Castillo el Collado €€€ *Paseo el Collado 1, Laguardia, tel: 945 621 200,* www.hotelcollado.com. This elegant, rustic hotel features ten antique-furnished rooms, which are individually styled on such themes as "Love and Madness", "The Cigar" and "Venus". There's also an intimate, top-notch restaurant.

Marqués de Riscal €€€€€ *Torrea 1, Elciego, tel: 94 518 08 80,* www.hotel-marquesderiscal.com. Designed by Frank Gehry and echoing his Guggenheim Museum, it is an extraordinary hotel, swaddled in a baffling tangle of multicoloured titanium ribbons. Laid out to offer beautiful views of the ancient village nearby, it's breath-taking, albeit smaller than you might expect. The 43 rooms themselves are large and opulent, but only half are in the main structure; the rest are set into the adjacent hillside. There are also two very classy restaurants.

Villa de Laguardia €€ *Hotel Paseo San Raimundo 15, Laguardia, tel: 94 560 05 60,* www.hotelvilladelaguardia.com. Large country-house hotel, a short walk south of the town wall, with light, spacious rooms and a good restaurant serving local cuisine paired with fine wines. Room type varies, but some of them have their own access to the thermal spa circuit.

VITORIA

La Casa de los Arquillos €€ *Calle de los Arquillos 1, tel: 94 515 12 59,* www.lacasadelosarquillos.com. Lovely little boutique hotel in a superb central location. Originally a medieval building, it is now converted to hold eight stylish en-suite bedrooms. They also offer eight larger but more expensive loft apartments in a nearby building. The one snag is that this area can get a little noisy, especially at weekends. Two-night minimum stay.

Dato €€ *Dato 28, tel: 94 514 72 30,* www.hoteldato.com. Beyond the gaudy mix of classical statues and gilded mirrors in the stairwells, this cosy hotel, close to the station, has super-helpful staff and tastefully decorated rooms with colourful batik bedspreads. All rooms have baths; pay a little extra for an enclosed balcony.

INDEX

INSIGHT GUIDES POCKET GUIDE

BILBAO

First Edition 2020

Editor: Aimee White
Author: Nick Inman
Head of DTP and Pre-Press: Rebeka Davies
Managing Editor: Carine Tracanelli
Picture Editor: Tom Smyth
Photography Credits: Alamy 5T, 40, 82,
85, 86, 88, 92, 96; Corrie Wingate/Apa
Publications 5MC; Dreamstime 52; Getty
Images 17, 19, 20, 24, 34; iStock 1, 4ML, 11,
28, 42, 46, 50, 54, 68, 72, 75; Public domain
23; Shutterstock 4TC, 4TL, 5TC, 5M, 5MC,
5M, 6L, 6R, 7, 7R, 12, 15, 30, 32, 37, 38, 41,
45, 48, 49, 55, 57, 59, 61, 63, 65, 67, 69, 70,
73, 74, 76, 78, 79, 80, 81, 91, 94, 100, 102,
104, 106; SuperStock 4MC
Cover Picture: Shutterstock

Distribution
UK, Ireland and Europe: Apa Publications
(UK) Ltd; sales@insightguides.com
United States and Canada: Ingram
Publisher Services; ips@ingramcontent.com
Australia and New Zealand: Woodslane;
info@woodslane.com.au
Southeast Asia: Apa Publications (SN) Pte;
singaporeoffice@insightguides.com
Worldwide: Apa Publications (UK) Ltd;
sales@insightguides.com

**Special Sales, Content Licensing
and CoPublishing**
Insight Guides can be purchased in bulk
quantities at discounted prices. We can
create special editions, personalised jackets
and corporate imprints tailored to your
needs. sales@insightguides.com;
www.insightguides.biz

Contact us
Every effort has been made to provide
accurate information in this publication,
but changes are inevitable. The publisher
cannot be responsible for any resulting loss,
inconvenience or injury. We would appreciate
it if readers would call our attention to any
errors or outdated information. We also
welcome your suggestions; please contact
us at: hello@insightguides.com
www.insightguides.com

Bilbao Metro

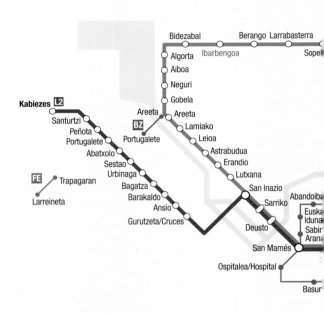

Bidezabal
Berango Larrabasterra
Algorta Ibarbengoa
Sopel
Aiboa
Neguri
Gobela
Areeta Areeta
Lamiako
Portugalete Leioa
Astrabudua
Erandio
Lutxana
San Inazio
Abandoiba
Sarriko
Euska
Iduna
Sabir
Arana
Deusto
San Mamés
Ospitalea/Hospital
Basur

Kabiezes L2
Santurtzi
Peñota
Portugalete
Abatxolo
Sestao
Urbinaga
FE Trapagaran
Bagatza
Barakaldo
Larreineta
Ansio
Gurutzeta/Cruces

BZ

Metro line

- **L1** Etxebarri – Plentzia
- **L2** Basauri – Kabiezes
- **L3** Kukullaga – Matiko
- ○ Stations
- ◎ Interchange station

TR Tranbia
(La Casilla – Atxuri)

FA Funicular Artxanda
(Artxanda – Castaños)

BZ Bizkaiko Zubia
(Portugalete – Areeta)

FE Funicular Larreineta
(Larreineta – Trapagaran)

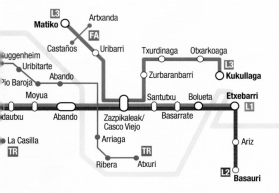

L1 **Plentzia**

Urduliz

L3
Matiko　Artxanda

FA

Castaños　Uribarri

Guggenheim　　Txurdinaga　Otxarkoaga
Uribitarte
Pio Baroja　Abando　Zurbaranbarri　L3 **Kukullaga**

Moyua　　　　　　Santutxu　Bolueta　**Etxebarri**
dautxu　Abando　　　　　　　　　　L1
　　　　　Zazpikaleak/　Basarrate
　　　　　Casco Viejo
La Casilla　　Arriaga　　　　　　Ariz
TR
　　　Ribera　Atxuri　　　L2 **Basauri**
TR

Plan & book
your tailor-made trip created by local travel experts at
insightguides.com/holidays

STEP 1

Pick your dream destination and submit an enquiry.

STEP 2

Fill in a form, sharing your travel preferences with a local expert.

STEP 3

Receive a trip proposal, which you can amend until you are satisfied.

STEP 4

Book securely online. Pack your bags and enjoy your holiday!